The Malt-Ease Flagon

In the Proverbs of Solomon you will find the following
words, "May we never want a friend in need, nor a bottle
to give him!" When found, make a note of.
—Captain Ned Cuttle

THE MALT-EASE FLAGON
Your Complete Guide to Home Brewing
Under American Conditions
(such as they are)

by R.O. Despain

TEN SPEED PRESS

Ten Speed Press
P.O. Box 7123
Berkeley, California 94707

Cover and Book Design by Brenton Beck
of Fifth Street Design Associates

Cover and Book Illustrations by David Omar White

Manufactured in the United States of America

Library of Congress Catalog Card Number: 78-24695
ISBN: 0-913668-87-7

To my grandparents, Lionel and Sarah, who raised six kids on seven-and-a-half acres and never made $1,000 a year. Of all my family, I think they'd best understand what this book is about.

Contents

Preface

What one fool can do, so can another.

—A. Nother

My fermenting career began back in the second grade of William Penn Elementary School near Salt Lake City, Utah. Our class was going to have a Halloween party and Richard, whose father had a cider press (capital machinery), Bill, whose father had an apple orchard (raw materials), and I (cheap exploitable labor) were assigned apple cider.

We got together after school and planned it: Bill and I would pick the apples and take them to Richard's house. Then, under his father's supervision, Richard would press the apples and take the cider to school on the day of the party.

While Bill and I were walking home, we got to talking about cider and hard cider. Our first thought was to harden the lot and get the class drunk. But our enthusiasm cooled when we realized that it would be difficult to pull off and that we were a cinch to get caught.

However, we did see that with a little lying we could at least harden enough cider to get ourselves drunk. We'd tell Bill's parents that we were supposed to bring three gallons instead of two. We'd pick apples for the three gallons, take a jug, and tell Richard's father that Bill's parents wanted him to press a gallon for them. Once we had the cider, we'd smuggle it home and go from there. Accomplished liars that we were, we pulled it off without a hitch.

Hardening the cider was another matter. We didn't dare ask grownups about it and we couldn't find any books we could understand. We ended up relying on instinct and hearsay (the whole process paralleled sex education in those primitive days).

We poured the cider into soda pop bottles and tackled our first problem: how to get the bottles closed without a capper and without corks. We'd learned in second grade how to make puppets out of papier-mache and it was simple to make stoppers instead. The bottles closed, we hid them in the floor joists over the furnace in Bill's basement. We then confidently went about our business, relying on Nature to do the rest.

It did.

When we'd worked up the courage to embark on our first drunk, we returned to the basement to find only fragments of glass reposing in pools of cider vinegar. No trace of the papier-mache stoppers has been found to this day.

More than twenty years later, when I resumed my career in brewing, I decided to get all the advice I could find. But inquiry failed to turn up a live tutor (maybe the legal situation had something to do with that), so I bought a book by mail-order. It was published in Great Britain, where homebrewing is legal, and, while doubtless useful to the British reader, it merely puzzled me with such advice as "nipping down to the corner chemist's for a bob's worth of sodium metabisulfite." I knew that the "chemist's" was the same as the drugstore, but I strongly suspected that if I went there and asked for anything more exotic than aspirin, they either wouldn't have it or would believe I was making bombs. I had nightmares of federal agents raiding the house to arrest a radical bomber and instead nailing me for bootlegging.

Still, by using the book, the brewing folklore picked up in twenty years, some common sense, and a lot of trial-and-error fooling around, I learned to brew. I made a lot of mistakes. Every time I made one, I took a note so that I could make a new mistake the next time around. By the time I could brew well, I found that I had a considerable store of notes.

Comparing my notes to the books, catalogs, and mimeographed sheets of one sort and another that I had added to my fermenting library, I was struck by how often the books made a great whoopdeedo about matters which were, once I got into them, simple, but neglected to warn me against real dangers or to tell me basic things—where to get brewing yeast, for example, or a capper or a hydrometer. My notes were more down-to-earth. I didn't want my hard-won experience to go to waste, but it came too late for me.

"I've already made every mistake in the book," I said to myself, falling into cliche.

Then it hit me: my mistakes *weren't in any book* on brewing I'd ever seen.

I decided to write that book.

This, I hope, is it.

R.O.D.

Ashford, Connecticut; Millcreek, Utah; Manoa, Hawaii.

CHAPTER I

You Brew, Too

God made yeast, as well as dough, and loves
fermentation just as dearly as he loves vegetation.
—Ralph Waldo Emerson

Brewing As Religion, Magic, Art, Science And Other Fancy Lies

You are interested in homebrew (or you wouldn't have picked up this book).

But everyone else seems to be interested in homebrew, too. The first time I taught a course on it, I expected ten, maybe twelve, people. We started out with sixty and grew to seventy-five as word got around. Some were driving as far as thirty miles one-way.

Everyone who finds out about my brewing asks me about it. When I think of the time I've spent gassing at gatherings where I could have used my mouth to eat or drink—or just could have kept it shut and listened—I have to shake my head.

But after all the talking I've done, I'm still left with this question: Why is it, that although everyone is interested in homebrew, so few brew?

Judging from what people have said, I'd guess that there are two main reasons. The first is that nearly everyone believes that brewing is so expensive, mysterious, complex, and dangerous that it would be impossible for anyone but a combination of J. Paul Getty, Sherlock Holmes, Dr. Linus Pauling, and a hardened, nerveless criminal—either a hit man or a real-estate agent—to pull it off.

When *you* brew, this belief can be gratifying. You casually let it slip out that you make your own booze and then stand around posing as a minor superman.

It is with some real regret, therefore, that I confess that it just ain't so.

You can buy the essential gear for around fifteen dollars. And instead of being weird, mad-scientist stuff—lembecs, telsa coils, vapor condensers—it has a homely, almost vulgar air about it: pan, turkey baster, bottle capper, siphon hose, bucket. Further, brewing isn't much harder than making stew. If you could teach monkeys to measure—and only crudely at that—they could make homebrew. In fact, the process is so safe and natural that most homebrewers do it while drinking or even drunk.

Brewing has been going on for about eight thousand years. Why hasn't word leaked out? The reason is simply that at all times it has been in the interests of Certain Powerful Groups that this truth be suppressed.

In the beginning, alcohol was a god and the gift of a god, its production and consumption, religious rites. Osiris gave beer to the Egyptians, Dionysus wine to the Greeks, and the coming of drinking wrenched Western society as violently as the coming of dopesmoking was to later. When looked at closely, all the hubbub in Euripides' *Bacchae* is the result of abstaining from and drinking wine in Thebes.

Once people started getting loaded in non-religious contexts, the monopoly of the priests was threatened. Surely it is no coincidence that such two-fisted drinkers as Socrates and Alcibiades, the chief protagonists of the archetypal drunken blast, Plato's *Symposium,* were ultimately both tried on trumped-up charges of impiety.

But even when consumption had become de-mystified, production remained bathed in a religious aura. Although their monopoly has long been broken, even today priests carry on the tradition. Go to the nearest package store and you will be reminded of the ancient connection by every shelf: from Benedictine and Chartreuse to Christian Brothers' California Brandy.

Perhaps it's because fermentation itself seems to duplicate and possess the greatest mystery of all—life. Something still and inert becomes a seething, frothy mass that slows, subsides, and dies away to Something once again inert, but utterly changed, transformed. Osiris and Dionysus are gone, yet even today most people believe down deep that fermentation is a form of White Magic. Perhaps it is.

By the time of the Middle Ages, production had largely passed from religious to secular hands but had once again become a near-monopoly. By 1406, for example, the brewers of London had formed the "Mistery of Free Brewers within the City" and were influencing legislation concerning manufacture, sale, and entrance into the trade by persuading the government that they alone had the skill to make proper brew. (Needless to say, this partnership between commerce and government proved so beneficial to both that it has continued to the present day.)

Proper brewing now required a kindly, old, roundcheeked, pot-bellied Brewmaster—a sort of Santa Claus, stuffed to the gills with arcane brewing knowledge learned at his father's knee. Thus did the "mystery" of brewing become first, the "mistery" and then the "mastery" as the sanction of Religion gave way to the sanction of Art.

But a further sanction remained. In these latter days, Science has reared its increasingly ugly head and has further de-mystified the production of beer. In the eighteenth century, Lavoisier explained the chemical change of sugars into alcohol and, in the nineteenth, Louis Pasteur explained the microbial aspects of both fermentation and its enemies. Although a full understanding of the enzymic reactions of fermentation wasn't reached until the 1960's, the commercial breweries were quick to alter the image of the Brewmaster. The craftsman, his clothes stained with malt, hops, and yeast, was scrubbed up and slapped into a white lab coat. Still milking the older image for all it was worth, the breweries now insisted that the Brewmaster— though kindly, roundcheeked, and pot-bellied—was a highly-trained scientist, stuffed to the gills with chemistry and microbiology learned at an Institute for Advanced Brewing Knowledge, a sort of super graduate school somewhere beyond the Ph.D.

Go to your local brewery (if it hasn't been put out of business by one of the big national firms) and you will be properly dazzled by precision dials and gauges, giant machines of gleaming stainless steel, and polysyllabic technological terminology. Once you've heard them tell you how expensive, mysterious, complex, and dangerous brewing is, you'd almost forget that deep in the wildernesses of Africa, South America, Polynesia, and Brunswick, New Jersey, people totally ignorant of Louis Pasteur, of *Saccharomyces carlsbergensis*, and of enzymes have been making brew for a hundred centuries.

The second reason people don't brew is that they're convinced that even if the process could be mastered, the results wouldn't be worth the effort. Those Certain Powerful Groups, when they will admit that homebrew exists at all, insist that it is vile, unhealthy, and inferior.

The situation is further complicated by the honest reactions of people who have been bummed-out at one time or another by bad homebrew. When my neighbor Bill heard I was brewing, for instance, he didn't take much interest in it. I invited him to come up to the house and try a bottle.

"What do you put in it?" he asked.

"Malt, sugar, water—stuff like that."

"No raw meat or potatoes?"

"Hell, no. What'd anybody want to put trash like that in?"

"I don't know, but Joe Ribly over in Westford used to make homebrew and he stuck in a chunk of raw meat and some potato slices while it was working."

"How'd it turn out?"

"Tasted like hell, but if you were plugged up, it'd do the job. One bottle and you were in the john for the rest of the night."

I explained that homebrew didn't have to work like that and, after drinking a bottle or two, Bill agreed. Before I get to answering the charges of those Certain Powerful Groups, I'd like to clear up any misunderstandings that may have come about if you or if someone you know has had a Bad Homebrew Experience. Try to bring the trauma back to mind and ask yourself. . .

Did the brew have exotic ingredients? Raw meat is, thank god, uncommon, but brewing folklore abounds in stuff that "must" go into homebrew. Simple, inexplicable legend accounts for some exotica, but others came about because earlier brewers lacked a ready source of brewing yeast and had to rely on wild yeasts. Raisins, other dried fruits, and potatoes are rich in wild yeasts and when added to the brew along with certain spices—ginger, for example—could get fermentation started. But keep in mind that anything needlessly added has a chance of adding a flavor you're not going to like and that wild yeasts can do very wild and unpleasant things to the aroma and taste of what otherwise could have been good homebrew.

Was the brew cloudy when you drank it? That cloud was made up of fresh yeast, which has a distinctive taste (I don't care for it) and is a mild laxative. Yeast is also said to add to the miseries of hangover.

How long had the brew been in the bottle before you drank it? If it was much less than six weeks—and beginning homebrewers being an impatient lot, it probably was—you were drinking *green* homebrew. The difference between green homebrew and homebrew is the same as between green fruit and ripe fruit. If the only cherries you'd ever had were small, hard, green marbles, you wouldn't think you *could* like cherries.

I won't deny that some things called homebrew by their makers are vile, but I will claim that once you know what you're doing, it's far easier to make good homebrew than it is to make bad. I've had at least a hundred people try mine—most of them close enough friends to tell me the truth—and every last one of them has genuinely enjoyed the homebrew experience. And no one has had to run for the john.

So much for claims of vileness. What about health? Let's fearlessly admit in front that alcohol itself is a protoplasmic poison. *All* alcohol—whether it's made by a monasteryful of pious and charitable monks high in the Alps or by a gang of greedy and merciless industrial distillers in the bowels of Chicago. That admission made, I'll go on to say that there is no form of alcohol less likely to injure your health than homebrew.

A bottle of commercial beer has beer in it, all right, but it can also legally have up to fifty-nine additives without saying a word on the label. Most, if not all, of these chemicals do nothing but enhance the appearance and the keeping qualities of the beer. There used to be sixty, but one of them, cobalt sulphate, killed a few people and the commercial brewers decided they'd better leave it out. They hate to lose paying customers (information from the Center of Science in the Public Interest via a column by Mike Royko, 6 March 1974).

You know exactly what's in homebrew because you put it there yourself. Water, sugar, lemon juice or citric acid, and salt are simple, basic, and safe. Malt extract, according to its makers "is a pure product of nature. . . . No chemicals, preservatives or artificial flavoring and coloring are used. . . ." I believe them. The preservatives in beer are there so that it can be shipped and stored for long periods of time without undergoing further change. If preservatives were added to malt extract, homebrewers would have to figure out some way to get rid of them so that the extract could be fermented.

The alleged inferiority of homebrew rests on two premises. The first is that *homemade* is inferior to *storebought*. Characteristic of (and perhaps necessary to) a highly industrialized society, this notion is at last rightfully on the wane. If you have any lingering doubts, find a friend who really knows how to cook Italian—slow simmered sauce that's made up with fresh spices bruised and added to taste and then is allowed to age for a few days; fresh homemade pasta rolled out of a noddle machine and cooked on the spot—and have that friend make spaghetti. Take along for comparison a can of Franco-American. If "spaghetti" wasn't written on the can, nobody would know what in the hell it was.

The second premise is that homebrew is homemade beer. It's not. But thinking so can keep you from finding out what homebrew is really all about. If you get set for something and something entirely different shows up, you're so surprised that you don't notice much about what did happen. If, for example, you're expecting to get milk and your glass has water in it, you'll usually gag or spit—surely not your normal reaction to water. If you're thinking beer, homebrew may surprise you so much that you won't be able to taste it.

So make no mistake: homebrew is vastly different from and vastly superior to ordinary commercial beer. People who don't like beer have accepted a glass of homebrew from me out of politeness and have discovered that they like it. When I've run out of homebrew and have been forced to substitute beer, I've always found it cheap and thin by comparison. But the difference and superiority of homebrew are not only a matter of flavor and taste but also one of effect. People who don't even like to drink have discovered—to their everlasting salvation—that they like drinking homebrew. You can go ahead and get drunk on it if you want to, but if you go about it right, homebrew has its own high (see *Advanced Drinking* in chapter VII).

Why Not to Brew

Now that I've disposed of the false reasons for not getting into homebrewing, I've got to admit that there are some real ones.

First, brewing may be illegal. Although several states have passed bills permitting homebrewing, the federal government, at this writing, has not. And federal law, which takes precedence over any state laws, provides for penalties of $10,000 and five years in the slammer for anyone fermenting malt or malt substitute to over one-half percent alcohol without permission—a rather strong penalty for such a weak brew. Word has it that the law is a holdover from prohibition days and is not being enforced at the present time. The IRS makes rumbling noises now and then, but no arrests.

The law may be unenforceable. Home winemaking is legal (even respectable: Sears sells kits for it). How sharply can a distinction be made between wine and brew? Since "malt substitute" can be anything that could substitute for malt—say, crushed grapes—anything fermented could be considered brew. Looking at the distinction the other way around we could say that since some wines are made from grains—sake from rice, for example—brew could be considered a sparkling wine made from barley.

If you plan to take advantage of this argument, see the *IRS* section in Appendix B. There are a few catches (some of which are being challenged in the courts), but if you're male, over 21, and married, you will routinely be given permission to make wine for home use.

What to do in the face of laws, penalties, and other inconveniences is up to you. To make a decision, you should consult your knowledge of your community as well as your conscience. As a rule of thumb, if you're the type on whom Federal Authorities have little or no reason to pay unannounced calls (i.e., if you look fairly straight in your neck of the woods), it's safe to brew. If the Feds come calling now and then, looking for Something Else, you must weigh the risk that not finding It, they may nail you for your brew.

As implausible as this scenario may seem, a recent court decision upheld a conviction for possession of marijuana which was found when police searched a house for explosives. Although the police had a warrant for only the explosives, the court ruled that they could act on whatever they found. An ominous decision (*Hartford Courant*, 27 January 1972).

But there may be an even more compelling reason for not brewing. E.B. White says that if you don't *enjoy* shoveling chickenshit, you'd better buy your eggs and leave chicken raising to someone else. Likewise, if you don't enjoy the process of brewing, leave it alone.

You can't be sure if you're going to like it until you've tried it, of course, but if you don't like mixing things or if watching bread rise leaves you cold, you'd better not get in too deep at first. If brewing becomes a drag, you're going to wind up with a basement full of empty bottles and with a few buckets of malt vinegar. You'll be better off to buy beer, no matter how much more it costs, than to save money at the expense of life.

The low cost of homebrew is a nice bonus for the committed brewer, but mere pennypinching, in any form, is damnnedly dull.

Why Not Brew?

If your enthusiasm has been dampened by all this negative argument, let me give you some of the reasons why I brew so you can see if they make sense to you.

First, as I've already said, homebrew is an excellent beverage, much superior in taste and effect to commercial beer. By making it, you control what goes into what you drink and how it's made. Homebrew is easily the safest, healthiest, most natural form of alcohol you can drink.

Second, homebrewing is the cheapest possible way to get smashed. Even after all these years of inflation, a pleasant, drinkable brew can be made for under ten cents a quart. If you drink on an empty stomach, you can get more than a mild buzz on for a dime, get very fuzzy for twenty cents, and get into the hospital for under a dollar.* Even when you're rather broke—I started brewing when my gross annual income was $2,000—you don't have to make your parties BYO.

Last, making something beautiful, delicious, and potent from a most unlikely looking, smelling, and tasting bunch of cheap ingredients is gratifying. It won't beat winning an Olympic Gold Medal or building a log cabin in the woods, but it gives the same kind of satisfaction.

Why Buy This Book?
(If You Haven't Already)

Learning to brew from a book—even a good book—is far from an ideal situation. Probably the best way to learn anything is to find people who know how and have them teach you. If you can find experienced brewers, by all means learn from them.

But buy this book anyway.

I'm not trying to placate my publisher or to rip off a royalty with this advice: as an apprentice, you'll learn to make your teachers' brews in their ways—a good thing. But this book will teach you something better: to make *your* brew in *your* way.

You're the only one inside your head. Therefore, only you can really know what you like. I know what *I* like and I know how to make it, but I've tried to overcome the urge to preach The One True Way (Mine). To be sure, I've told you how I brew and why, but I've also told you other ways to try and maybe to adopt. In fact, to avoid forcing The Perfect Brew down your throat, I've started you out with a recipe I seldom use and I've told you how to change it.

Although the Table of Contents should have given you a good idea of what's in the book, I'd like to explain a little further. The first two chapters try to give you a good picture of what brewing and what learning to brew from this book will be like. After having read them,

---

*Inflation has been raising hell with my attempts to get this book finished. I put the penultimate draft aside to cool for a month while I earned my living and came back to find the price of sugar tripled. But even today, you can make a quart of homebrew for twelve-and-a-half cents. I've changed money estimates so many times that I'm worn out. No more.

Besides, the absolute prices are less important than this simple fact: the price of manufactured beer always goes up faster than the price of its ingredients. Therefore, the more inflation inflates, the bigger bargain homebrew becomes.

you should pretty well know whether you want to continue or whether you should wrap the book up and give it to someone else.

Chapter III tells you (in some detail) what you'll need and how to get it. You start simple so that if you change your mind later, it'll have cost you as little as possible.

Chapter IV also tries to stay simple. After a short section on theory, you'll find a basic recipe and the procedures to brew, to explore what you've made, and to change the recipe to what you want — *Your* Perfect Brew. I've given you a lot of detail as to what to expect as you go along; these details aren't necessary, but they should keep you from worrying about what the yeast are doing.

Chapter V contains advanced procedures. Once you've got the basics in Chapter IV under your belt, you can try whatever interests you here.

Chapter VI treats cooking with homebrew. By no means an exhaustive collection of recipes, it also should take you to the point where you can decide whether you want to go on or not.

Chapter VII is a catch-all.

What I Hope This Book Is About

Independence. Partially from the cash economy and our economic system, completely from commercial breweries, and ultimately from this book itself.

Freedom. Not to randomly fuzz around, but to find what *you* want and to get it.

CHAPTER II

A Digression on Bread

*I don't know why it should be a crack thing to be a
brewer; but it is indisputable that while you cannot
possibly be genteel and bake, you may be as genteel as
never was and brew. You see it every day.*

—Herbert Pocket

I said earlier that if seeing bread rise leaves you cold, you might not
like brewing. You could make a practical test since I have a bread
recipe and a few further analogies between breadmaking and brewing
up my sleeve. At the same time, you can try learning from this book
with no outlay for equipment and very little for materials.

In contrast to the trial-and-error experience by which I learned
to brew, I first learned to make bread from a booklet intended for 4-H
girls. The booklet wisely assumed that the reader didn't know
anything about baking and therefore described each step in considerable detail. Since I was working on my own and was, at that
time, completely innocent of the mysteries of yeast, as well as those
of the kitchen, the booklet's assumptions proved crucial: had it
assumed more, I would have been confused and might well have
failed.

If at times I seem to be over-explaining the obvious, both in this
chapter and elsewhere, I hope you will understand my intentions and
forgive my verbosity.

From the points of view of ingredients and procedures, the
bread you're going to make is about the simplest kind possible. I make
it in French-style loaves and find that its chewy, thick crust makes it

particularly good for eating hot from the oven and for dipping in fondues.

The first step is to get a mixing bowl that will hold eight cups or more. Put in two cups of *warm* water.

Question: What is *warm* water?

Your respectable uptown cookbooks will tell you that water used with yeast *must be between 105° and 115° F.* If we miss and the water is only 104° F., we are to believe that the yeast will sit in the puddle of cold water and do nothing. Similarly, if the water is 116° F., the yeast are supposed to perish from the heat.

Common sense warns us that this state of affairs is unlikely and experience and a little work with a thermometer show that the cookbooks are wrong on this particular point. I've made bread using water ranging from about 80° to 120° F. and my yeast have managed. Water from my cold water tap is a little under 70° F. and from the hot water tap, around 120° F. I suspect that most water systems run about the same, although a good hot water heater can deliver 145° F. (I keep the thermostat on mine turned down to save fuel). Since you're not going to try to get *warm* water from the cold tap or from the hot tap (after it has been running full blast for awhile), any water you can get from the taps that *you think is warm* is going to work. Although baking yeast may work optimally at 105° to 115° F., such precision is unnecessary for making bread. If you *think* it's warm, it *is*. It's as simple as that.

We find the same situation in brewing. Any number of books and people will tell you that if you don't brew *exactly their way,* your bottle will explode, destroying the house. What brew survives will turn to sour vinegar which will poison or at least blind you.

Nonsense. Brew (like tribal lays) can be made in hundreds of ways and every one of them is right. In fact, brewing is so simple and natural that it's impossible to go far wrong if you use simple common sense.

Back to the bread. Add two teaspoons of salt, a tablespoon of sugar, and an envelope of yeast. Give the yeast time to soften and then stir to dissolve everything. Put in three cups of plain, unsifted white flour and beat the mixture with a wooden spoon until everything is stirred up and the batter shines a little. Once you get the flour mixed into the water, it won't need much beating.

Stir in more flour, adding about half a cup at a time. Depending on the weather and the kind of flour you use, you should get something between a cup and a half and three cups more stirred in. Don't worry about knowing when to stop. When it's time, the flour you add will just sit there on the bottom of the bowl and the dough will become so stiff that you won't be able to stir it anymore anyway. Even if you do stop too soon or too late, you won't be making a mistake, as you'll see a little later.

Kneading the dough comes next. Sprinkle some flour around on your working surface and turn the dough out of the bowl. Fill the bowl with hot water and let it soak. Rub some flour onto your hands, sprinkle some on the dough, and start to knead it. As the dough gets sticky, sprinkle more flour on it and on your working surface.

People develop individual kneading patterns as they gain experience—this is mine: I press the dough out into a flat circle. Then I grab the upper right-hand third with my right hand, fold it over on top of the dough towards the center, turn the dough a third of a turn, and lean into the fold with both hands to press the dough into a circle once again. I'm right-handed; left-handers might try reversing the directions.

Knead the dough for at least seven minutes by the clock before you let yourself wonder if it's been kneaded enough. This will keep your tired muscles from short-circuiting your good intentions. There are a number of ways to tell when you can quit. You can look at it and stop when all of the raw flour has been kneaded in. I tell by the feel of the dough—when it gets smooth and satiny; by the process of kneading—when the dough doesn't seem to want to stick together when I fold it over; and by my hands—when they don't get sticky as fast.

Retrospect: Mixing bread, from the adding of the first flour until the kneading is completed, is a *single* process. The division into parts is more for the convenience of the baker than for the good of the bread. Therefore, *there is no need to worry* about whether you've completed one part of the process correctly. If you don't stir enough flour into the batter, you'll knead it into the dough. I know of one person who misread a recipe card and added one half cup of flour to the batter instead of two and a half cups. The dough, when it was turned out of the bowl, was very sticky, to say the least. But after the person had kneaded in enough flour to be satisfied, the dough was exactly the same as it would have been if more flour had been stirred in to start with. The bread was good.

While brewing, you can find a great deal to worry about as you go through the various processes. Fortunately, if you keep doing the work, your worry won't hurt the brew at all. If you need to think about what's going on, keep this in mind: you are the minor partner in a natural, symbiotic relationship that was established 10,000 years ago. Yeast have a life of their own. They want to make brew; it's their nature to do it. Your job as a human is often no more complicated than staying out of their way and letting them do what they want to.

Back to the bread again. When the dough has been kneaded, set it aside and take a plastic scouring pad or a dish cloth to the mixing bowl, which has been soaking in hot water. The water makes the dough soft and easy to clean up, so a few swipes should do the trick. Rinse the bowl with hot water and dry it.

Grease the bowl with shortening, margarine, or butter (the cheaper, the better—that's why shortening is listed first) and put the doughball into the bowl. Tip the dough out again, turn the newly greased side up, and put the dough back in the bowl. Cover the bowl with a piece of waxed paper or a piece of plastic wrap and then with an ordinary dish towel (or an extraordinary dish towel if you have one). If you make the piece of plastic wrap a little longer than the loaves are going to be, say about 18 inches, and then fold it in half to cover the bowl, you can use the same piece to cover the loaves later.

You are now ready to rise the dough.* Once again we hear rumblings from the cookbooks advising us that the dough must double in bulk in a draft-free environment maintained at a temperature between 80° and 85° F. This means, of course, that breadmaking is possible only during a few windless summer mornings and evenings or in a greenhouse.

Once again we ignore the advice and use our common sense. I've discovered that the dough is going to rise—despite the cookbooks—almost anywhere in the kitchen. As long as you don't chill it by sticking it in the fridge or don't try to cook it by putting it in a heated oven, it's going to rise. I put mine on top of the stove near the pilot light, but I do this more to have it near the stove timer than to seek an 82.5° F. location. The unheated oven is a good place, too.

"Double in bulk"—that ominous phrase should give us pause. The average person is a very poor judge of volume (as I discovered when I tried to estimate how much fill I was going to need to build a walkway and some flower beds). To estimate accurately by eye the relative volumes of two highly irregular spheroids (one of which exists only as a memory) bounded by truncated paraboloids of revolution is a feat not to be undertaken lightly. A good grounding in analytical geometry (if not, vector algebra) should be the minimum prerequisite.

---

*Raise the dough, except in the sense of "to get cash up," is a good example of a usage error known as *overcorrection*. The use of *rise*, an intransitive verb, is tacit linguistic recognition that the yeast are doing the real work.

The dough is rising relentlessly and we require a year's course in higher mathematics. What to do?

We can do one of two things. First, this task has proven even too much for orthodox cookbooks and so science has had to give way to folklore. Their recommendation is to "press the tips of two fingers lightly and quickly one-half inch into the dough. If the dent stays, it is double." (What if you slip and push .505 of an inch?)

But if you have better things to do than to hang around the kitchen poking dough at intervals (and then measuring your poke), just set the timer for about an hour and forget about it. When the timer rings, you can try poking the dough if that will ease your conscience.

The next step, punching down, is a massive poke anyway. Punch your fist into the center of the dough. It's good for you. Let the doughball represent the sources of your current frustrations, take a good windup, and POW! As the dough collapses, pull the edges of the ball over to the center crater, turn the doughball out on your working surface, and knead it a little to get more of the gas out.

To form loaves, begin by cutting the dough in half. I use a knife with a serrated edge and cut slowly, trying to make the two halves come out even (they rarely do). Pat the halves into balls and let them rest for about five minutes. While they're resting, get out a baking sheet (or anything else about that size that can go in the oven) and grease it with whatever you used on the bowl. Roll the balls into loaves—just the way you used to make snakes out of clay in kindergarten—and put them on the baking sheet. If you want lots of chewy crust, for fondues, for example, make the loaves long and thin. If you don't, make them short and fat. Cover the loaves with the waxed paper or plastic wrap and the dish towel and let them rise for another hour.

When they've risen, you can uncover them and make diagonal slashes on the tops of the loaves if you want to. The loaves then go into a 425° F. oven for 25 minutes. You can then take them out, brush them with egg white, and return them to the oven for five minutes more. When the bread's done, the crust will be a nice tan and the loaves will sound hollow when you tap them with your fingernail.

When I started making this bread, I slashed and egged, but it soon occurred to me that it was a lot of trouble. The slashes and the egg white coating looked nice, I guess, but they didn't help me cut the baked loaves and they didn't seem to have anything to do with the taste of the bread. Moreover, I usually managed to burn my fingers while trying to brush on the egg white. I now let the loaves bake for 27 minutes unmolested, check them, and sometimes let them bake a minute or so more.

Similarly, when I'm brewing and I wonder whether to add something new or to try some new method, I go ahead and try it a couple of times to see what difference it makes to the brew. If it makes little or none, but the procedure is fun or the ingredient is cheap, I keep doing it. (If you enjoy slashing your loaves, don't let me dissuade you.)

Obviously, if the new thing makes little or no difference and it's a pain to do or costs an arm and a leg, that's that for that. The crunch comes when it does make a difference in the brew and it's extra grief. I let H.D. Thoreau be my guide and try to figure life costs. Usually I forget about it or try it now and then when I feel up to it.

Once you've made the bread, please re-read these instructions. Unless I'm mistaken, you should notice that making the bread is, in fact, much easier than trying to understand the instructions. This is one of those universals of experience that keep life from being simple: doing something you know how to do is, of course, easy; learning how to do something by doing it is only slightly harder; but understanding how to do something from reading or hearing about it (or even seeing it on TV) is significantly harder. If Adam and Eve had been required to read and understand a bunch of marriage manuals before they could try any of it out, there would be little demand for bread—or brew—now.

So don't mistake the difficulty of understanding my contorted prose for difficulty in brewing. If you don't fully understand the directions, use your common sense and go ahead with your brewing. You'll soon find your way, even if you never understand whatever fuzzy-headed chain of reasoning I was after: there are fathers who believe to this day that storks bring babies.

If you keep on making bread, you'll soon find out how unnecessary my directions are. You'll finish kneading the dough, not because you make the tests I've outlined, but because you'll just know that the dough has been kneaded enough. In fact, if you have to explain how you know, you'll have to sit around and think about it for some time, just as I had to do in writing this chapter. Likewise, experienced bakers know when the dough is ready to be punched down, but they can't tell how they know, so they come up with this lame business about "doubling in bulk."

Similarly, when you've become experienced in brewing, you'll come to the stage when you know what you're doing without having to think about it. If you bother to re-read this book, you'll wonder why I was making such a to-do over such a simple and natural process.

One last piece of advice, and then we'll be through with bread. If you want to acquire a reputation as a talented cook, a generous person, and, at the same time, someone at once earthy and mystical, just take a loaf hot from the oven and give it to your neighbors now and then.

Of course, it's all rot. Cooking talent? Well, I'd rate bread right in there with competent mud-pies—decent scrambled eggs are much harder. Generous? Fifteen cents a loaf. Earthy? Mystical? You'll have to judge your own case. But there is such a mystique about baking one's own bread that mere facts must give way to it. Consider: a loaf of store bread costs fifty cents. Buy some and give it and some scrambled eggs to your neighbors. Even though you've been much more generous, etc. than if you'd given homemade bread, they'll think you're just trying to pull something.

Store-bought beer will be met with less resistance, perhaps, but the general principle holds true nonetheless. If you give away some of your homebrew, however, you will become a popular, if enigmatic, person in your neighborhood.*

---

*If you sell it instead of giving it away, you may become a *marked* man in your neighborhood (see Chapter I).

CHAPTER III

Getting Your Kit Together

Had I but a flask of gin,
Sugar here for two,
And a great, big bowl for to mix 'em in,
I'd pour a drink for you,
My dear Mary Anne.

—Mary Anne

When I started brewing in earnest, my biggest problem was finding out what I really needed in the way of equipment and ingredients and then finding out where to get them. My guides were a British book on brewing and my accumulation of brewing folklore. The book told me that everything I needed could be found at the local corner store. The folklore told me I had to get such exotica as a giant crock. I wasted a lot of time asking after things like brewing yeast in grocery stores and getting nothing but suspicious looks.

I also wasted money buying things I didn't need. As a result, I can make a rough estimate of what this chapter is worth to you in cash. My brewing gear cost me about thirty-five dollars. Yours should cost you about fourteen dollars, maybe seventeen (two of which are due to inflation). By making use of my abundant capacity for error, you should be able to save about twenty bucks—maybe a little less, depending on the mistakes *you* make.

Shopping

Let's start with a few common-sense rules that apply to most buying situations.

    1. Shop around and watch for sales. I've found identical boxes

of bottle caps selling for 69¢ and 49¢ in two stores that weren't a block apart.

2. Make sure you can't get something locally before you send off for it. In addition to shipping, some mail-order outfits have a way of charging more, perhaps because they count on things not being available locally. That 49¢ box of caps cost $1.44 from a mail-order brewing supply place in the same state.

3. Think about substituting things you have or can get for things you don't or can't. The mail-order places are hot to sell you a jim-dandy, all-glass wine thief for around $2.50. The turkey baster that you either borrow from the kitchen or buy down at the grocery store for 69¢ will do the job just as well.

4. Consider sharing with another brewer (or brewers). Each of you will need some items—like a vat—but others—like a capper—are put to only occasional use and can easily be shared. If you can talk just one other person into going into homebrewing, your equipment should cost each of you around eight or nine dollars.

Cooperation has other obvious advantages: you can sometimes save by buying in bulk; some operations, like siphoning, go better with just a little help; and two (or more) heads are better.

I've dealt with equipment first because buying it tends to be a one-shot deal and because having it on hand gives you the security to get the ingredients and begin brewing. Before you go shopping, it would be a good idea to read this chapter and chapters IV and V as well. The reading should give you an idea of what gear you want to get and you may save trips and postage by getting it all at once. (But keep in mind what I've said about not getting in too deep at first.) For each item, I've given you the easiest/cheapest source, but I've tried to give alternate sources as well to keep from hanging you up if my best pick doesn't pan out. Good hunting.

Capital Equipment

Vat. When all's said and done, if you have something to brew and something to brew it in, you can do without the rest. That's why I begin with the vat. When I started in brewing, I automatically looked for a crock. I had some vague impression that without one, the brew either wouldn't ferment, or, if it did, would be dangerous. Fortunately, I couldn'd find a crock and I soon discovered that I really didn't need one and didn't want one. If you have a crock, well and good, but you might consider the advantages of some of the other vessels before you decide to use it.

Your vat shouldn't be made of metal.* While stainless steel is all right, if you can afford to get a tank big enough to be of practical use, you're rich. Hire a brewing tutor. Everyone else is limited to glass or plastic.

Glass has the advantage of being transparent so that you can watch your wort working. It has the disadvantages of being heavy and expensive. Further, the only vats possible from the points of view of availability and cost—carboys—are difficult to clean.

Plastic has the advantages of being cheap, light, and easy to find. You can get all kinds of good vats at any discount department store.

Once you've decided what size you want, arm yourself with a tape measure, some paper, a pencil, and this fact: 1 gallon = 231 cubic inches. You may want to review your solid geometry, but generally, two formulas will do the job. Volume of a cylinder = 3.14 r^2h, where r is the radius and h the height. This will do for estimating the volume of buckets, garbage cans, and circular wastebaskets. You can treat almost everything else as a rectangular solid and multiply the three dimensions for the volume. If it has slanting sides, take your measurements about half-way up and keep in mind that you don't have to be very precise. You have to make these elaborate preparations because plasticsware is irregularly labeled and sales clerks don't know. What's worse, they bluff and lie if you ask them about volumes (for estimates of volume, by eye, see chapter II).

Regardless of what size batch you intend to brew ultimately, I'd recommend looking for a plastic pail that will hold three gallons or a little more. This is about right for the two and a half gallon batch in chapter IV. Even if you're planning for bigger batches, you can use this pail for transferring. Two and a half gallons—twenty pounds—is about the most you'll want to try to carry up and down the cellar stairs.

After looking around for awhile, I found a pail that has a good handle, holds a little more than three gallons, has quarts and gallons marked on the inside, and that usually costs a little over a dollar (I've seen it advertised at various specials and plastic riots for 79¢).

If you're planning bigger batches, I'd advise you to scout wastebaskets and garbage cans. Try to find one with a lid that fits securely but isn't airtight. If the lid is airtight, you'll have to fix it so that the

---

*Every brewing rule has its exception. The Bantus brew in iron pots and, as a result, never suffer from anemia. If they had to haul those pots up and down stairs from the cellar to the kitchen, though, they might suffer from hernia.

carbon dioxide from fermentation can escape, or you could wind up with a split vat. If anaerobic brewing interests you (see chapter V), you could install a fermentation lock on an airtight lid and be all set. Because you've got to leave two to four inches of space for the brewing head, you'll need a vat that holds more than your intended batch size.

If you can't find anything to do the job locally, or if you want something super-posh, check the mail-order catalogs (see Appendix A for an annotated list). They have a number of goodies ranging from heavy crocks (the postage alone would buy you a good garbage can locally) to polyethylene vats with airlocks and spigots already attached.

If you've been brainwashed to the point where you can't get along without a crock, I'll tell you all I know about getting one. First, you can try whatever junk or antique shops you can find. If you find a crock, make damn sure the glaze is perfect. Cracks make the crock impossible to clean and a dirty crock can spoil a batch. Next, you can try to find some place that sells them new. I never did find such a place in Connecticut, but when I was a kid in Salt Lake City, you could buy them from a place that outfitted uranium prospectors, river runners, sheepherders, and other crazies. A restaurant supply house makes sense, too. Last, you can shoot your wad on mail-order.

Siphon. Home brewers have used everything from garden hoses to douche bag tubing, so you have a wide variety of stuff to choose from locally. I found some ⅜ inch clear vinyl tubing for about 12¢ a foot that I like because I can watch the brew as I siphon. Seeing it coming can save you from gagging on an unexpected mouthful.

The only real requirements are that the tubing be flexible enough to work around whatever obstacles you have in your layout, that it be small enough to fit inside whatever you put your brew up in, and that it not react with the brew. If you can't find clear vinyl tubing (I found mine in a surplus store), you might try surgical rubber tubing, especially if you know someone who works at a hospital.

How much to get? The amount required varies inversely with the ideality of your brewing layout. If you have a special shelf for your vat right above a special shelf for your bottles, you could use as little as three feet (or twice the depth of your vat). Slightly less than ideal conditions could be handled with six feet, average conditions with about eight feet. I have ten.

Hydrometer. Finding a hydrometer is easier now than it was when I got started in brewing. Mail-order was the only way then, but now you may be able to find a local amateur winemaking shop. Try the underground or college paper or the yellow pages. If you find a hydrometer locally, check specs and prices against mail-order. Specialty shop mark-ups can be pretty stiff and once you figure sales tax vs. postage, etc., you may save money by buying through mail-order. On the other hand, the shop has it now.

When you find a source for a hydrometer, you're going to be dazzled by the number of models available. Which one to get? Basically, all hydrometers measure one of or a combination of three things: specific gravity, sugar content in terms of degrees Balling (or Brix), and potential alcohol. Every one I've come across measures one of the first two and throws in the others if the maker wants to. Converting from one scale of values to another is *easy* (see the table in Appendix C), so if you can get a single scale hydrometer for less, go ahead.

If you're going to be making wine too, you may as well get one hydrometer to do both jobs. Since 14 percent alcohol is the upper practical limit for home winemaking, a range of 1.000 to 1.110 specific gravity, or 0° to 26° Brix or Balling, is adequate, although most hydrometers go well beyond. If you're getting only into brewing, you can get a brewing hydrometer, which may have a narrower range and a red line to tell you when to bottle.

You have one further decision: whether to order your hydrometer with a test jar or not. If you can read your hydrometer at zero in your brewing vat, and if you intend to ferment *only* in the vat (see chapter V), you can get along without a test jar. Otherwise, get one and get a turkey baster (or thief) to draw off samples for it.

Most hydrometers are advertised as coming "packed in a plastic tube that can be used as a test jar." That's true, but there's a problem. The plastic has a property called "thermal memory." With time and heat, the plastic tube remembers when it was part of a coil of tubing and tries to return to that shape. When it gets curved enough, it won't work as a test jar anymore. I'd advise starting with the plastic tube, keeping it straight by avoiding long, hot-water soaks, and scouting around for a glass replacement (chem lab supply room, etc.) to use when the tube gets irreparably bent. A good graduated cylinder could be used both as a test jar and for making precise liquid measurements.

Hydrometer prices vary. The most I've seen asked for a hydrometer and test jar is $5. I bought a triple-scale, wide-range (0.990 to 1.700 SG) hydrometer in a plastic tube for $2.50 because it was the least expensive I could find (it pays to shop around). Inflation has inflated since, of course.

Strictly speaking, a hydrometer is unnecessary. I've explained in chapter IV why I believe you should start with one, but if you can't find one or if you don't want to spend the money for one, read the section on *priming* in chapter V and brew without. Most of the brewers in the last 10,000 years have had to do without, but have found it no real hardship.

Capper. There are two kinds of capper in common use: the "Jet" capper (about $6) and the rack-and-pinion ("Everedy") type (about $8-9). The "Jet" grips the crown of the bottle and forces the cap on. With the "Everedy," you set the bottle on the base, and a racked plunger, driven by the pinion gear, forces the cap on. The "Jet" is more convenient on a single bottle or on a few bottles of mixed sizes; the "Everedy" is easier and faster on large batches or when the bottles are all the same size.

A third type, the "Climax," can occasionally be found in junk shops, attics, and basements. It looks and works like a bumper jack. A handle-and-plunger moves on a notched upright and forces the cap on the bottle. I've never used one, but I'd say that they'd be about the same as the "Everedy."

You can get cappers from Sears mail-order, the mail-order outfits listed in Appendix A, and sometimes locally, although many stores carry them as a summer item only. But . . . BEFORE YOU BUY A CAPPER, LOOK INTO THE LOCAL BOTTLE SITUATION.

Bottles. Sad story: When I was getting into brewing, I was fatally attracted to Imperial Quarts. They were nicely shaped of thick, heavy, brown glass—in short, ravishingly beautiful. I saved them through all the months it took me to locate a rack-and-pinion capper, finally buying one in an old, run-down department store in the center of the city.

When the time came to bottle, I lovingly placed a filled Imperial on the base of the capper and noted with rising alarm that the plunger was all the way to the top. Although I fiddled a full fifteen frustrating minutes, finally there was no way I could get a cap between the top of the bottle and the plunger. Yes, the Imperials were just one-eighth of an inch too tall. Utter incompatibility.

I cried a lot, then swore a lot, then grit my teeth and sent off six bucks for a "Jet" capper. Since it grips just the crown of the bottle, it can handle Imperials.

Moral: Make sure the capper you buy will fit the bottles you can get.

Sadder story: Back when "no deposit" bottles made their first appearance, a winemaking friend of mine thought of them as heaven-sent, religiously collected a heap of them, and trustingly filled them with his new wine. The treacherous bottles waited until he had left for Italy and then committed suicide, dumping the wine on his cellar floor.

Moral: If it has a price, you can pay from your pocket; if it's "free," you'll pay from your hide.

Another friend, who worked in a commercial bottling plant, tells me that "no deposits" are equally prone to spontaneous explosion when filled with tame soda pop. He says that on warmish and hot days, old bottling plant hands go far out of their way to avoid passing filled "no deposit" bottles. They never know when they'll be trying to duck a curtain of flying glass fragments.

If this doesn't convince you, take a "no deposit" bottle and an Imperial Quart (or just a plain deposit bottle). Look at them, measure the thickness of the glass, heft them, take them down to the cellar and throw them at the wall. If you were in a typical barroom brawl armed with one of the freebies and hit someone over the head, he'd only know about it by the sound of the tinkling glass. The Imperial is a no-shit, deadly weapon.

Most "no deposit" bottles are unusable for yet another reason. Believing the typical American beer drinker to be either too lazy or too stupid to operate the typical American beer opener, the beer manufacturers provide twist-off caps. Twisting the twist-offs back on won't hack it because the metal is too soft to make a good seal. Your capper won't put a new cap on them either, so twist-offs are doubly worthless.

Still, I know brewers who use them, even though they run the risk of winding up with flat brew when the caps don't seal or with broken bottles when they do. But, in good conscience, I just can't recommend these freebies.

Good, brown, heavy, deposit beer bottles are what I recommend and, even though you have to pay the deposit, they're "freer" in the long run than the "no deposits." In fact, they may represent something of an investment. A local long-time dealer in junk and antiques, recently sold a number of nineteenth-century Connecticut bottles for about $125 each. Although demand in the antique market depends on how many people share an obsession for the same junk, your deposit is a rock-bottom, guaranteed price that can always be collected by you (or your heirs).

Now that you're sold on the heavy bottles, I'll admit that you may have some problems getting them together. A local package store is probably your best bet. If you don't see what you need, ask, and the manager can probably get something from one of his distributors. I even confessed to my package store manager that I wanted the bottles for homebrewing and even though he realized that he was eventually going to lose one of his case-buying customers, he was nice about it. I guess he figured that the sudden windfall before my buying dropped off to nothing was better than having me go somewhere else to buy my last cases.

When I moved to Hawaii, I was unable to find deposit beer bottles. Asking around did no good. The distributors have an isolated captive market and import from the mainland what they please—cans and twist-offs. I was able to buy 20 ounce Foster Ale bottles from Australia and Kirin beer bottles from Japan, but the stuff in the bottles was so expensive, that I rounded out my collection with deposit soda pop bottles. These aren't as handy as standard quart beer bottles: They're taller and more of a nuisance to store and their shape isn't as good for pouring the brew off the yeast (see chapter IV). But they'll do.

The future availability of deposit beer bottles is highly uncertain. They're very unpopular with bottle makers and with beer and soft drink manufacturers. On the other hand, they're very popular with people who like drinking beer but don't like litter. In Oregon, where a law was passed in the fall of 1972 requiring deposit bottles, the price of beer has dropped and on a sample 25 mile stretch of highway, litter dropped from 3,037 cans and 921 bottles to 252 cans and 157 bottles. But anti-ecology forces have been gaining strength (did you notice how much harder the oil "shortage" hit Oregon than Washington?) and as of today, the outcome of the battle is still in doubt.

The beer manufacturers may be preparing a sneaky flanking movement that will hit homebrewers particularly hard. A wire-service report from Manchester, New Hampshire, says that Rheingold Brewers, Inc., has been testing a new 12 ounce deposit bottle that won't take a cap. Twenty-four of these little cheapies come in a case with a *higher* deposit than the 12 quart standard case, so it looks doubly bad for us.

Where will it all lead? It looks as if the presently little-used, sturdy, big, cheap, cappable deposit bottle may be replaced by a mandatory, flimsy, small, expensive, unresealable (outside of a beer factory) deposit bottle. We can only hope that some mechanical genius is working on a home device that will allow us to at least close the twist-offs, flip-tops, or Fug-A-Jugs that the manufacturers are going to spring on us next.

Making homebrewing bottles: If you get good deposit bottles already filled with beer (or soda pop), you still have to make them into homebrewing bottles. The procedure is simple. First, drink the beer. Last, the instant the beer is out of the bottle, rinse it. I half-fill my bottles with hot water, shake them around to dissolve anything that's left, pour the water out, fill them all the way up with hot water, and let them sit for a while. I then pour out half of the water, give the bottles another good shake and swirl, and pour out the rest of the water. If the bottles are going to sit around empty for more than a few days, I put small pieces of aluminum foil over the tops as caps to keep out dust, spiders, and wild yeasts.

If you follow this Rinsing Ritual as compulsively as a raccoon, you can put your homebrew into the bottles with no further cleaning. The beer factory does a good job of getting them clean before they put their stuff in them and if you're prompt and careful, the bottles will stay clean. If you're drunk or lazy and let the bottles sit around with beer in them, the beer will grow such slimy things as are beyond belief or description.

Salvaging beer bottles: After you've bought a few cases of beer for the bottles and made some homebrew, you may find yourself thinking: "Beer costs seventy-five cents a quart and brew only 12; therefore, if I could somehow get bottles that were empty to start with, I could have six times as much to drink for the money."

You will thereupon start canvassing grocery and liquor stores and taverns, looking to get cases of empties for the deposit. Since bottles cost beer manufacturers far more than the deposit, they discourage these kinds of deals, so be prepred to meet resistance.

Motivated as much by love of finagling as by greed, I once out-flanked the skeptical grocers, shopkeepers, and bartenders by getting fifteen cases of empties from a distributor's warehouse through labyrinthine string-pulling. As I stacked the cases in my basement, I gloated in triumph.

My joy was shortlived. In an average case of twelve bottles, two had cigarette butts floating in leftover beer, four had various kinds of molds growing on the sides and bottoms, and six were just dirty.

Cleaning up on these bargains requires one to two hours of detailed, sweaty work per case. I begin by examining each bottle carefully, sorting into three categories: *ciggies, moldies,* and merely *dirties.* The *ciggies* are dealt with first. Empty them into a bucket and give them a quick rinse. Inspect again and reclassify. Although cigarette butts smell terrible and look worse, they seem to inhibit the growth of mold; most if not all of your ex-ciggies will go into the dirties.

The *moldies* come next and require far more attention. Begin by trying to remove the mold mechanically. I go through the rinsing ritual vigorously, inspecting the bottle at the end of each step. If you have a large number of bottles to deal with—and if your luck is like mine, you will have—you can save time and water by using a funnel and pouring water from one bottle to another during each step. I usually work with three or four bottles at a time. This procedure, supplemented now and then by a few well-directed strokes with a bottle brush, will clear about half of the bottles of mold. Transfer the cleared bottles to the dirties and put the others aside for later treatment.

You've noticed that except for the unresponsive moldies, all of the bottles end up as dirties. Divide the *dirties* into lots of six (more or less) and go through a modified rinsing ritual. Half-fill the first bottle and shake it very thoroughly. Pour the water through a funnel into the next bottle and shake it, pouring the water into the next bottle in turn. After you have gone through all six bottles, half-fill the *last* bottle in the string with fresh water and do the same thing again. Keep pouring and shaking, changing water at the end of the string, until the water looks clean.

When all of the bottles have been rinsed, make up a sterilizing solution of one-fourth teaspoon sodium meta-bisulfite and one-fourth teaspoon citric acid in a quart of water. Half-fill the first bottle in a string of twelve, shake lightly, and pour into the next bottle to continue the procedure. When you have rinsed the last bottle in a string, distribute the used solution among the recalcitrant moldies.

Next, fill each clean bottle all the way up with water to drive the SO_2 fumes out. Again, one bottleful of water and the judicious use of your funnel will save time and water. My bottles next go into the dishwasher for a 145° rinse and dry (I use a partial cycle). If you don't have a dishwasher, rinse the bottles with boiled water which has been cooled enough not to break them.

The old moldies, now containing the used sterilizing solution, become *soakers*. Store them until you work up the strength and nerve and sinew to tackle another batch of bad bought bottles. Then pour out the solution (not down the john if you have a septic system) and treat them like (sorry) new moldies. If you collect a whole case of completely unrepentent soakers, make them look the best you can, take them down to your local package store, trade them in on a case of beerfilled bottles, and make homebrewing bottles following the procedure given earlier in this chapter.

A vat, a siphon, a hydrometer, a capper, and some bottles are the only special items of equipment you need to get started in brewing. Other equipment is needed, of course, but the items are few and easy to find: a pan or kettle, a wooden spoon or some other big stirrer, a funnel, a measuring cup, some measuring spoons, a plastic scouring pad, and some rubber bands. Look in your kitchen.

Raw Materials

Nevertheless, wheat for man, and corn for the ox, and
oats for the horse, and rye for the fowls and for swine,
and for all beasts of the fields, and barley for mild drinks,
as also other grains.
　　　　　　　　　　　—Doctrine and Covenants, 89:17

The situation with ingredients is much the same as with equipment. Some things you have on hand, some you can find locally with a little searching, and some you'll have to get through mail-order. I've suggested alternatives to help you find things and also to give you ideas for later experimentation.

Water. Certain commercial breweries make a great deal of hoop-de-do over the qualities of their water. Other breweries, located in less scenic parts of the country, never say a word about it, but go into ecstasies over some other gimmick. Let's face it: water does make some difference, but since you're not going to have yours shipped in from Tumwater, Washington, or a high Rocky Mountain spring in Colorado, you'll have to make do with what you've got.

Start at the cold water tap in your kitchen. Unless the water tastes nasty, you can probably stop your search right there. When I lived in rural New England, I had my own well and pump. The water from the tap came straight from nature and it was delicious. In Hawaii, where I live now, the water has been tinkered with by various agencies of the federal, state, county, and city governments. I still use it right from the tap. Some homebrewers, however, let treated city water stand overnight, boil it, or both, to try to improve the taste. I'd recommend giving these techniques a try only after you've done some brewing. Then you can compare results.

If the water from your tap does taste nasty, you have a problem. One solution is untreated water from somewhere else. Most communities have a legendary spring or artesian well that flows for all takers. When I was a boy, the nearest one was about two miles from the house. My father says that back during Prohibition, when everyone was into homebrewing, the fountain always had a long line of people patiently waiting to draw water—even in Salt Lake City.

If you can't stand your tap water and you can't find free spring water, you might consider buying bottled water.

Sugar. Start with plain, white sugar from the grocery store. When you're ready to experiment, you can branch out to invert sugar, brown sugar, corn syrup, molasses, honey, maple sap, or whatever source of sugar you'd care to try.

Invert sugar is a hotly debated issue among homebrewers (you'll find the details in the next chapter). I've brewed with it, but I've never noticed a difference worth the extra trouble or expense. If you want to try, you can either buy corn sugar, which is invert, by mail-order or invert the white stuff you buy in the grocery. The procedure is explained in chapter V.

Malt. The easiest malt to get and use is the extract you should be able to find in your local grocery store. Folklore has it that large chain groceries carry it when you can't find it elsewhere. If you don't see it on the shelves, ask the manager before you give up. They hide it in strange places: I've found it coyly nestled next to the Ovaltine in one store and honestly standing up with the beer in another.

If the store managers say they don't know anything about it, write to

Premier Malt Products, Inc.
1137 N. 8th Street
Milwaukee, WS 53201

and tell them your problems. They'll put you in touch with their local food broker and either the broker will tell you where to buy the malt extract or you can tell your grocer who to order it from.

The malt extract, Blue Ribbon brand, is hop-flavored and comes in four kinds: Pale Dry, Extra Pale, Light, and Dark. I've run on to every kind at one time or another, but I've never seen more than two kinds in any one grocery store. Start with what you can get; if you have a choice between the dark and one of the lights, pick the light unless you've had pleasant experiences with dark beer.

Mail-order outfits stock a variety of other malt extracts, both in syrup and dried form. They cost more and they have to be shipped, but there they are.

If you want to take the process back a step, you can buy malted grain by mail-order and extract it yourself. I've never done it and I don't intend to until I can get malted grain as easily and as cheaply as extract. Hardier souls will find instructions in chapter V.

You can even go one step further back and malt your own grain. Again, you'll find the procedure in chapter V, but since this chapter concerns procurement of raw materials, let me lay one further caution on you here. You'll be malting seed barley. If you don't grow your own (the only sensible reason for getting into malting anyway), you'll probably get it from a grain and feed store. READ THE LABELS CAREFULLY. It has become customary to treat seeds with all manner of chemicals for all manner of reasons. None of the chemicals will do you any good and one of the commonest, mercury, can make you as mad as a hatter—see your annotations to *Alice in Wonderland*.

Yeast. Flat recommendation: start with genuine bottom-fermenting, lager yeast. You'll probably have to order it by mail. I buy dried brewing yeast in foil packets. Twenty cents worth is good for two small batches or for one larger batch—up to twenty gallons. Dried yeast stores very well and is easy to use.

Don't be tempted by baking yeast or brewer's yeast tablets by their lower cost or their availability. These yeast can ferment sugar to alcohol but they have several practical drawbacks. First (and least important), they can't stand as much alcohol as regular yeast. Second, brews made with these yeasts don't clear as well. They may leave a slight yeast haze, which is displeasing to the senses of sight and taste (but see chapter I for the *effect* of fresh yeast). Third, and most important, these yeasts don't stick to the bottom of the bottle as firmly as regular yeasts do. This means that yeast will start to come over into your glass or pitcher much sooner when you pour the brew. Either you settle for a lot less or you have to put up with a lot of yeast in your brew.

So for the trifling difference in cost, it's better to leave baking yeast in the kitchen and brewer's yeast tablets for the anemiacs and get yeasts intended for the job. If the cost still strikes you as excessive, see the suggestions for stretching yeast in chapter V.

Bottle caps. If you bought your capper locally, try to get caps at the same place. Make sure they stock them year round or make sure you buy enough to get you through the winter. If you've made a friend of your grocery store manager while buying malt, try to get him to stock caps. Or you can try any store that carries homemade root beer extract. If all else fails, you can buy caps through mail-order.

Hops. If you use hop-flavored malt extract and stick with light-bodied brews, you may find that you'll never need to worry about hops. But if you want them later, the cheapest (and probably the best) form is the fresh compressed package that you get by mail-order.

Others. Yeast nutrient helps yeast do the job. Various kinds are available by mail-order. Citric acid helps fermentation and gypsum is a water treatment. Both may be available locally and both can be bought through mail-order. Neither is absolutely required. You can use lemon juice instead of citric acid and just leave gypsum out.

Sympathetic grocery store managers are very useful in getting raw materials. They'll help you with special orders for cases of malt extract (and may give you a case discount) or see that extract and bottle caps are kept in stock. The next time you go shopping, meet your grocery store manager and size her or him up. Most of the ones I've met are extremely nice people.

If your grocery store manager is unsympathetic or you live in a paranoid state like Utah,* you may want to exercise a little judgment and restraint. Space your purchases out: don't stack twenty pounds of sugar, four cans of malt extract, and two boxes of bottle caps on your cart and head for the register. You may get home to find the ward teachers or the sheriff waiting on your doorstep.

---

*How to tell if your state is paranoid: get a Sears mail-order catalog and find the ad for their winemaking kit. Will they ship it to your state? If not, figure that your state is at least a trifle paranoid and watch your step.

CHAPTER IV

Basic Brewing

Cool head main t'ing.
—Pidgin saying

These next two chapters are organized so that beginning brewers will progress naturally from innocence to wisdom. After a short stretch of theory to remove brewing from the realm of white magic and to enable you to understand why you do certain things, I give a recipe for a simple, light brew with a moderate amount of clout. Since this brew is something like most commercial beers, it won't require you to change your tastes instantly in order to appreciate it.

The procedures that follow the recipe are effective, simple, and straightforward. But they are *my* ways and I promised to teach you to brew *your* way. To do it, I've added comments on alternative procedures as I go along, together with occasional bits of theory so that you'll know the consequences of changing a given procedure.

However, the main tool for learning to brew *your* way is the last procedure in this chapter, *Changing the recipe.* Here you'll learn how to educate your taste for homebrew and how to change the recipe so as to satisfy your developing conception of The Ultimate Brew.

In the next chapter, I deal with more radical changes and alternatives to the procedures in this one. I recommend staying here until you have a good feel for what's going on. Then tackle whatever you think is worth a try in chapter V.

Theory

Fermentation is chemical change brought about by microorganisms, chiefly yeasts and bacteria. If all yeasts came in foil packets, like baking and brewing yeast, making homebrew would be a simple process. But, to make things more interesting, wild yeasts and other microorganisms, including the feared acetobacters, are normally present in the air and on exposed surfaces. Our basic brewing strategy, then, is to control conditions so that brewing yeast, *Saccharomyces carlsbergensis*, can carry out its intention of turning sugar to alcohol and carbon dioxide:

$$C_6H_{12}O \qquad 2\ C_2H_5OH + 2\ CO_2$$

At the same time, we want to keep wild yeasts from starting (most of them cause off-tastes), but above all, we want to stop the acetobacters, whose perverted desire is to seize the alcohol made by our good yeasts and turn it to watery vinegar:

$$C_2H_5OH \qquad CH_3COOH + H_2O$$

Brewing yeasts can work either aerobically—taking oxygen from the air—or anaerobically—taking oxygen from the sugar—and they like temperatures between 55° and 85° F. Acetobacters are strictly aerobic and like temperatures around 85° F. and higher. Wild yeasts have their own preferred range of temperatures. All microorganisms work slower at colder temperatures, eventually becoming dormant, and faster at higher temperatures, although a high enough temperature—145° F.—kills them.

These few simple facts underlie all brewing practice.

Basic Recipe

So much for theory. Here's the basic recipe with approximate costs. Since inflation seems inevitable between the time I'm writing this and the time you'll be reading it, everything costs more now.

Bob's Basic Bucket Brew (Ten quarts)

Amount	Ingredient	Cost
As needed	Water	$ .00
4½ cups	Sugar	.50
½ tsp	Salt	.00
½ tsp	Citric acid (or juice of one lemon)	.02
1 cup	Malt extract	.55
1 tsp	Nutrient	.03
½ package	Brewing yeast	.15
	Total cost:	$1.25

Basic Procedures

Making up. The first step is to assemble and dissolve the ingredients. The resulting stuff is called *wort*. Get a large pan and put 2 to 4 quarts of water in it. Warm the water and dissolve the sugar, salt, and citric acid. (If you're using the juice of a lemon instead of the citric acid, add it after the wort has cooled.)

Next you're going to add the malt extract, which will sink like mud to the bottom of the pan. To avoid a burnt taste in the finished brew, turn off the heat and let the pan cool a bit.

It's easy to write "measure out one cup of malt extract," but it's tricky to do. If you have a new can, the extract will be fairly pourable, but still very thick and viscid. Your problem will be to make it stop pouring when you have one cup. I'd suggest pouring slowly into a two-cup measure and, when you estimate that enough is in the air between the rim of the can and the measuring cup to get up to the one cup mark, interrupting the flow with a table knife. If you act firmly and swiftly and if you're lucky, you won't wind up too sticky. Put an aluminum foil cover over the can of malt and put it in the refrigerator.

The second and subsequent times around with a can, you have to take it out of the fridge and heat the can in water to soften the malt so that it can be poured.

Pour the measured malt extract into the pan and stir endlessly until dissolved. If your measuring cup is dishwasher proof, you can stick it in the pan and rinse it with hot wort to dissolve the last vestiges of malt. You may also add boiling water to the measuring cup, stir it around, and pour everything into the pan.

Thriftiness is not the only reason for going after every last smidgen of malt extract; once it cools and hardens, it's a bear to clean up. You may as well make a little extra effort to see that the malt goes into the wort rather than having to be scraped out of the cup later.

When all is dissolved, you can either pour the wort directly into your vat, or you can play it supersafe by first heating it to 145° F. and keeping it at this temperature for one-half hour to kill all of the wild and incidental yeasts. Add as much water as you can (without winding up with more than ten quarts of wort) and use a candy thermometer to measure temperature. I usually don't play it safe since both the extract and sugar have gone through something like this during manufacture and my water is fresh out of the well.

When you have the wort in the vat, add enough water to make ten quarts. If your vat doesn't have its own markings, it's an easy job to make your own. Scratch them on the inside, if possible, so that you can see the level of the liquid come up to the mark. If it's not possible, try putting tape on the outside and pressing against it with your thumbnail to make a dent on the inside to measure with.

Put a piece of plastic over the top of the vat, securing it with a string of rubber bands and let the warm wort come to room temperature. If you have a candy thermometer, you can clip it on the vat and keep a watch. I did the first time, but I soon grew tired of watching the temperature not go down. Now I let the wort stand overnight and judge by touch.

When the wort reaches room temperature, stir in the yeast nutrient.

Pitching yeast. Different forms of brewing yeast require different handling. Some, particularly the liquid ones, have to be started well ahead of time by putting them into a solution of nutrient and sugar and getting them to begin fermenting. Dried yeast is easy to use. For a ten-quart batch, measure out a scant teaspoon (half of the package), sprinkle it onto the surface of one-half cup warm water (see chapter II if you're in a quandary as to what *warm* water is), and let it soak for ten minutes.

This is a good time to take an initial hydrometer reading since the yeast foam interferes once the yeast is pitched. The initial reading should be around 1.050 to 1.055, but don't get upset if it isn't. As long as you're close (1.030 to 1.070), you'll come out all right. Stir the yeast (it may be foamy, but if it's grainy and lumpy instead, that's no cause for alarm), and then stir it into the wort.

Fermenting. Your part in the fermenting is to find a good place for the vat and then to keep a cool head while the yeast do the work. What constitutes a "good place" is another of the subjects that gets homebrewers into arguments. To *my* way of thinking, an *ideal* place would be clean, draft-free, and would maintain a temperature of 60° F., steady as a stone. Most brewers go along with cleanliness and draft-freeness and agree that the temperature should be constant. *What* that temperature should be forms the center of the dispute.

A "good place" means, of course, a good place for the brewing yeast to do their work and a poor one for the harmful micro-organisms to do theirs. If a place is clean, there is less chance for wild yeasts and acetobacters to be present in the first place. A steady temperature helps friend and foe alike. If the temperature varies a lot, microorganisms, our yeast included, stop doing their jobs and just sit there (confused, probably). This condition, called a "stuck" fermentation, can lead to loss of the batch unless the fermentation can be restarted (see the section on *Saving mistakes* in the next chapter).

Our yeast starts with three advantages over the bad guys, particularly acetobacters. The plastic cover over the vat gives us two of these, first by keeping out foreign microorganisms and, second, by keeping in the carbon dioxide that is being given off. The CO_2 forms a protective blanket over the wort, cutting off air. Thus, although the anaerobic good guys can keep doing their stuff, the acetobacters lack the oxygen to do theirs.

The third advantage is that we choose a temperature at which the yeast thrives, but that acetobacters find a little too cold. Once the fermentation gets well under way, we gain a fourth advantage from the alcohol that's being produced. Although the acetobacters lust after it to turn it to vinegar, too much of it disables them. Kind of like humans.

I've heard that brewing at lower temperatures is good also because the yeast concentrates on making simple alcohols and stays away from higher alcohols and esters that cause off-flavors and may add to the miseries of a hangover. Higher brewing temperatures mean faster fermentations, but the risk of haste making vinegar is increased (for details, see *Driving* in the next chapter).

So much for ideal conditions. Real conditions can vary all over the lot without preventing fermentation from taking place. In the summer I brew in my cellar, which maintains a fairly constant temperature of around 65° F. Towards early fall the temperature drops to where I'd have to wait almost forever for fermentation to finish. When this happens, I move the vat into my study, which I keep at around 67° during the day and 60° during the night. In the spring, I've had some classical stuck fermentations because of rapid and wide changes in temperature (like 80° one day and a blizzard the next). A friend brews outside during the summer in a thirty-gallon crock and takes his chances. So far, he hasn't had trouble. You can probably brew wherever you have space—provided the temperature is reasonable—and expect to get by.

Keeping cool while the yeast works probably helps you more than the yeast. However, the less you're monkeying with the vat, the less chance there is of wild yeasts getting in and spoiling things. Judging from my experience, I'd say you're not running much of a risk anyway.

You have two tools to help keep you cool: your hydrometer and your developing knowledge of what to expect from the wort as it ferments. Recommending using a hydrometer from the beginning may seem to be a deviation from my avowed purpose of keeping things as simple as possible. Most of the books on brewing recommend exactly the reverse: begin *without* the hydrometer (since it's hard to get and not necessary), then use one later when you've gained experience.

Since I was waiting for my hydrometer to arrive by mail, I made my first two batches without one. Wondering whether the wort was stuck or not, whether the fermentation was over yet or not, or even how far things were along during those few months of optimism when I believed the wort *was* fermenting, took much time and energy. Learning to use a hydrometer seems much more simple to me than trying to know without any prior experience where the wort is at. Further, by using the hydrometer, the beginning brewer can avoid having to prime completely fermented wort.

Using the hydrometer is a very simple matter anyway. Put the hydrometer in its test jar and use your wine-thief (or turkey baster) to suck up wort from the vat. Tip the test jar and let the wort run down the side to prevent foaming. Filling the jar almost to the top makes reading the hydrometer easier, but all you need is enough wort to float the hydrometer. The next step is to get the hydrometer floating freely, not touching the bottom or the sides of the jar. The easiest way to do this is to hold the jar so that it's vertical with one hand and shake the hydrometer with the other hand (to get bubbles off). Then spin it. It will come to rest in the center of the jar and you can take your reading.

How often should you take hydrometer readings? In the beginning, you should take one whenever you feel the psychological need. As long as the readings keep coming down, you know fermentation is taking place. After you get experience, you'll probably take an initial reading and then put away your hydrometer until the wort is very nearly finished. The readings will decrease slowly at first as the fermentation starts up, then rapidly, and then slowly again as the fermentation nears its end.

Knowing what else to expect during fermentation also helps keep you cool. The book I had on brewing kept leading up to an explanation of what was going to happen, but never got there. As a consequence, everything was unexpected and no matter what happened, I felt obliged to worry about it. After I'd brewed a successful batch or two, the former alarming indications that I was headed for vinegar or worse became instead familiar signposts on the road to alcohol. You'll probably do the same trip, but to ease your mind now, let me give you some idea of what to expect.

At the beginning, the wort will look like thick syrup or gravy and smell like a wet gunny sack. If you taste it, expecting it to taste like beer, you will be disappointed. It tastes a little like a wet gunny sack and it's very sweet since the sugar is unfermented. At this point it's difficult to believe that anything worth drinking can come from the wort.

After the yeast has been pitched, the time it takes for fermentation to start and the rate at which it will proceed depends mainly on the brewing temperature. The warmer the temperature, the quicker the start and the less time it will take the wort to ferment. At more-or-less average temperatures (yeah, I'm hedging), the wort will just sit there and do nothing for anywhere from four to twenty-four hours. It's easy to convince yourself that your yeast are no good or that you've killed them through improper handling or of any other horror show that may flit through your mind. At the end of this nerve-wracking period, very small dots of white foam will begin to appear on the surface of the wort. My first impulse was to fear that something —insects? fruit flies? spiders?—was attacking the wort and would soon have it spoiled. It was, of course, the yeast beginning their work at last.

The dots will grow into a large, white brewing head flecked with gray or brown spots. Don't worry about the spots; they're yeast and/or stuff from the malt. (Don't worry if there are *no* spots.) The brewing head will stay around anywhere from a day to a week and then disappear as the fermentation slows, leaving the surface of the wort fairly open. There will be spots of light foam and, in the open areas, small bubbles of CO_2 gas coming to the surface will make it look like a mud puddle in a light rain storm. An exceptionally ugly brown ring of yeast and godknowswhat may form around the top of the vat. Depending on the type of yeast you've used, you may have a layer of it floating on top of the wort. Don't worry about it.

Once the brewing head disappears and the fermentation slows down, you'll want to start taking hydrometer readings so you'll know when to bottle. A reading of 1.005 or the "B" or red line on a brewing hydrometer means that the wort contains just enough unfermented sugar to produce the desired amount of CO_2 in the finished brew. Getting it right is important. If you leave too much sugar to ferment in the bottle, the excess carbon dioxide gives you gas later. If there's just a little too much, the bottle will foam violently when you open it, possibly running over the side and stirring up the yeast on the bottom. The effect ranges from mildly annoying—an inch of brew with a five-inch head—to not being able to drink the brew without getting a lot of fresh yeast. If there's too much CO_2, the bottles blow up.

If you leave too little sugar to ferment in the bottle, the brew will be flatter than normal. You have some leeway, but take care with your last readings and if you're going to make a mistake, bottle later rather than earlier. (Once you've made a mistake, whichever it is, see the section on *Saving mistakes* in the next chapter.)

It's nice to be able to bottle just as the fermentation runs its course and the hydrometer reading gets to 1.005, but it's not always possible. Sometimes it's the middle of the night, sometimes you're away from home, and sometimes you just don't feel like it (particularly with large batches). It is always possible, however, to bottle at a reading of 1.005. If you're ready, but the brew isn't, wait. If the brew's ready, *prime* it back to 1.005 by adding sugar. This can be tricky; directions are found in chapter V.

Bottling. If you like to see such virtues as foresight, fidelity to duty, and industry rewarded, this is the place. Those who have faithfully followed the Rinsing Ritual prescribed in chapter III will now have clean bottles ready to be filled with brew. Everyone else must first clean bottles.

If the bottles are fairly decent—no mold, no vinegar, no rock-hard deposits of dried beer—and if you have a dishwasher, you can get by with only minor grief. Put the bottles in the dishwasher, select the 145° cycle, and switch to the beginning of the last rinse. Let them rinse, dry, and cool. If you don't have a dishwasher and the bottles are *very* decent—clean but dusty on the inside—you can get by with chemical sterilization. Make up the sterilizing solution given in chapter III and follow the directions for its use. If your bottles are less than decent, turn to the section on reclaiming bottles in chapter III, follow the directions, and resolve to do better in the future.

Once you have clean bottles, the rest is easy. Carefully siphon the brew from the vat into the bottles, leaving one-half to one and a half inches of space in the bottle. Don't use a ruler to measure; just get the brew up into the neck. If you use your right hand to put the siphon into the bottles and if your siphon hose is fairly flexible, you can control the flow by pinching the hose with your left hand. Pinching slows the flow down but doesn't cut it off completely; you'll wind up with less brew on the outside of the bottles if, as one bottle is about filled, you shift your eyes to the neck of the next bottle, squeeze with the left hand, and smoothly transfer the siphon with the right.

Siphoning goes better with one person for each end of the siphon. One fills the bottles and the other keeps the suction end of the siphon just below the surface of the wort in the vat and cuts off the bottling when the heavy yeast sediment at the bottom is reached. If you siphon some of this yeast into the bottles, don't worry. It'll have a chance to settle out later.

When the bottles have been filled, cap and label them. I put a piece of masking tape on the cap and write a batch number on that. Others scratch on the cap or stamp the date with a small rubber stamp.

Cleaning up. Wet yeast and wet wort are like mud and water—easy to clean. Dried yeast and dried wort are like lichen—you almost need to pry or blast them loose. You can save three-fourths of the work by not delaying it. Rinse your brewing tools and containers right after you empty or use them.

Avoid soap and detergents. They can wind up either affecting the taste of what you brew or adding some foam you're not going to like. The best thing I've found for cleaning is baking soda. I put in a good dollop and let things soak. The second best thing for cleaning is a woven plastic scrubbing pad. You don't have to use soap with it and it rinses clean.

The best thing to do with your vat after you bottle is to rinse it out, pour the yeasty sediment down the toilet (it's said to do good things for your septic tank), and begin making up a new batch. That way, there's no chance of a little disregarded brew turning to vinegar and lying in wait.

Conditioning. Place the bottles upright in cases and store them at warm room temperature for about a week. Play it safe by putting the cases someplace where spilled brew won't be a disaster. I've used the broom closet and the bathroom. The warm temperature encourages the yeast to ferment the rest of the sugar, producing the CO_2 to carbonate or "condition" the brew.

After bottling and while fermentation continues, the brew will look something like apricot nectar—cloudy and almost opaque—because of yeast and other matter being kept in suspension. When fermentation finishes, the yeast and the other stuff will form a layer on the bottom of the bottle and the brew will become brilliantly clear. It's not necessary to buy any of the various "clarifiers" stocked by the mail-order houses. Properly made homebrew clarifies itself.

Aging. The brew can be drunk as soon as it clears—usually within five to ten days. However, it will taste acid and sharp—"green" is what brewers call it, probably by analogy with fruit. Aging improves brew greatly—almost beyond belief. It will improve at a very rapid rate for about two months and then at a slower rate up to a year. After that, it starts to go down hill, slowly at first and then rapidly. You can age the brew anywhere you have space to store the bottles upright, except someplace where they could freeze and break.

I've discovered a few aging rules of thumb, all of which seem to be special cases of Emerson's Law of Compensation. First, cooler aging temperatures take longer, but seem to do a better job. Second, pints and smaller bottles age faster than quarts, but quarts seem to age more thoroughly. Third, the more complex, exotic, or alcoholic the brew, the longer it's going to take to age to the point where it's pleasant to drink.

Drinking. Carefully take your bottles from storage and put them upright in the fridge to cool them to serving temperature. The idea is to pour off the brew and leave the layer of yeast sediment behind. Pop the cap and pour the brew very slowly into a chilled glass pitcher or stein in one careful, continuous process, stopping when you see the heavy yeast getting set to come over. Set the pitcher down, and, even before you think of drinking the brew, RINSE THAT BOTTLE.

Use the pitcher to fill glasses. Avoid plastic pitchers and glasses. Plastic has a porous surface that causes the brew to overfoam as it flows by. I serve my homebrew in wineglasses because it's pretty and fun to watch. In addition to being wonderfully clear—commercial beer looks muddy by comparison—homebrew has thousands of tiny bubbles very finely dissolved throughout the liquid. Because of the natural method of conditioning by fermentation in the bottle, homebrew looks more like very good champagne than it does commercial beer.

Drink it. If you're new to it, don't be put off by the fact that it doesn't taste like beer. Suspend your judgment of what it's *supposed* to taste like, and *taste* it.

Changing the Recipe

Here we are. I'd suggest two or three experiments to educate your taste before you start seeking The Ultimate Brew. First, use two cups of malt and cut the sugar by a cup. Take and record the initial potential alcohol reading so you can take it into account when you compare. It should be around the reading for your first batch. You should now have one cup of malt extract left in the can, so make up another batch following the basic recipe.

Buy a new can of extract, selecting a new flavor—dark if you've used light or pale for your first batch. Make up a batch using the basic recipe and then a batch using two cups of malt and cutting the sugar. This should give you five batches: 1) basic recipe, light malt; 2) double light malt; 3) basic recipe, light malt, but greener than the first batch; 4) basic recipe, dark malt; 5) double dark malt. As these batches age, you'll be in a position to explore differences in age, body, and flavor.

Differences in *age* are obvious to taste but hard to put into words. Green homebrew has an "edge" to it and you seem to taste a number of distinct flavors individually but also at the same time. As the brew ages, the edge vanishes and the flavors blend into a single entity. Try a side-by-side comparison test between your first and third batches and you'll taste what I mean, even though you might disagree with my description. The overwhelming probability is that you'll prefer the more aged of the two brews.

Body is even harder to describe. If you compare your first, second, and third batches, you'll be able to taste a difference in age, of course. But when you've had enough experience with age to discount the difference, you'll notice a further difference between the second batch, on the one hand, and the first and third, on the other. This is body. Body is usually described in terms of weight: the second batch has "heavier" or "fuller" body than the first or third. The sense of body seems partially muscular and partially gustatory.

Flavor is a familiar and straightforward concept. Compare batch two to batch five and batch three to batch four. Light and dark.

There are at least two other factors that you can control by changing the recipe (or by your timing of when to bottle). The first, *clout,* is roughly proportional to the percentage of alcohol in the brew and determines how drunk you're going to get on a given volume in a given time. The second, *condition,* is the amount of carbonation in the brew and depends on the hydrometer reading at which the wort is bottled. Condition also changes with aging. Even after the brew clears, fermentation is taking place at a very slow rate. I've found that a brew that seemed rather flat after five weeks in the bottle had developed a good head and a lot of bubbly by seven or ten weeks.

You're probably ahead of me by now, but let me sum up how changes in the final brew come about. *Body* is determined by the *proportion* of malt extract to sugar in the wort. The more malt and the less sugar, the more body. Some brewers take the view that you should use *only* malt and that sugar is just a cheap filler. It's the law in Germany, so if you like German beers, you might try adding malt and cutting back on sugar till the sugar's all gone.

Flavor is a complex matter. The kind of malt determines the basic flavor of the brew. But since the malt extract is hop-flavored, the more you use, the more hop flavor and total flavor you're going to have. You can also change the flavor by using different kinds of sugar. Brown sugar contributes a rather distinctive taste, so I'd advise you to start out with just a little added to the regular white sugar and find out if you like it before you try an all brown sugar batch.

Since both the malt extract and the sugar get turned to alcohol by the yeast, the more total malt and sugar you have, the more *clout*. By taking an initial hydrometer reading, you can always know how alcoholic your batch is going to be. The basic recipe yields five to seven percent alcohol, which is respectable. Trying to brew much above ten percent potential alcohol is asking for trouble. The yeast find the going tougher and a change in temperature that would be all right in less alcohol can stick your wort. Further, it will take the more alcoholic brew longer to age to where you want to drink it. Less is more.

If you're looking to make liquid dynamite, brew up some seven or eight percent stuff and follow the directions for *jacking* in the next chapter.

You can control the amount of *condition* of the brew by bottling at different hydrometer readings. There are serious risks if you miss, so take it in easy steps, say increments of .001 degrees SG.

Overall, homebrewers seem to start with pale malt extract and light body and get darker and heavier as they go along. If you go this route, you'll probably find a point at which something seems to be missing. A good brew has to have *balance* and an old rule of thumb says the more body you have, the more bitterness and hop flavor you need. You get both from adding hops to your brew. That takes us to the next chapter.

CHAPTER V

Other Ways

> PUEBLO, Colo. (AP) — Sheriff Joe Torres has denied
> that County Jail prisoners operated an illegal still inside
> the jail, but he did admit that inmates had used potato
> peelings mixed with yeast and water to make alcohol.
>   This fact was discovered when a prisoner was stabbed
> with a knife during a drunken brawl in County Jail.

After you've got a good feel for the basics, you'll be ready to try using some variations with ingredients, or increasing your rate of production to keep up with increasing demand, or even adding some other beverages to your repertoire. These and other matters are taken up in this chapter.

The organization of this chapter moves from procedures carried out early in the process of brewing to those carried out late. The first group has to do with ingredients and all of the work is done before making up the wort. The second group deals with procedures during fermentation and afterwards, including a section on what to do when disaster seems to have struck. The last group deals with brewing in larger batches and with producing things other than brew.

Dealing with Ingredients

Using hops. Hops, as you recall, add flavor and bitterness to your brew. If you want to try using them, I'd suggest starting out by adding one ounce to the double malt recipe.

Hops present two problems. First, they're physically something like loose tea. While you want to extract flavor, you don't want to wind up with a lot of soggy plants in your brew. Second, the bitterness that hops add comes from highly volatile oils. If you're careless, you'll lose the oil.

Hops come in compressed blocks weighing from two to eight ounces. I measure the hops by measuring the block with a ruler and then sawing off what I need with a knife. However you go about getting what you need, wrap the rest of the block in aluminum foil. Break the hops up and wrap them in cheesecloth. If you could find a giant tea-ball or sew a sack out of something with a loose weave, that would probably do as well. If you have trouble finding cheesecloth at the grocery, try the paint section of your local hardware store.

Put enough water in a pan to cover the hops (don't add them yet; just estimate) and bring it to a full boil. Reduce the heat, add the hop sack, and cover the pan. Let everything boil gently for a half hour and then turn the heat off and let the pan cool covered. By keeping the pan covered at all times until it's cooled, you keep the bitter oil from escaping. When the pan has cooled, remove the lid, squeeze the hop sack, and pour the hop tea into your vat. That's it.

Inverting sugar. Ordinary sugar, as you may remember from high school chemistry, is a mixture of simple sugars, *monosaccharides,* and complex sugars, *polysaccharides,* which are chains of monosaccharides. Before yeast can convert sugar to alcohol, they must first break the chains down into the simpler monosaccharides. Some brewers argue that if invert sugar, which is made up entirely of monosaccharides, could be given to the yeast to start with, they could get on with the job of brewing right off the bat.

You can buy invert sugars, but you can also invert ordinary sugar without too much trouble. Dissolve the 4½ cups of sugar called for in the basic recipe in 18 ounces of water. Add three-fourths teaspoon of citric acid (or the juice of one lemon). Bring the mixture to a boil slowly, stirring as necessary to dissolve the sugar. Let it boil gently for a half-hour without stirring and then cool. Pour it into your vat and you're ready to go.

If you like the results of using invert sugar, you may as well make it in large quantities. A five-pound sack of sugar will require two teaspoons of citric acid (or the juice of two lemons) and should be dissolved in 2½ cups of water. Store the syrup in the refrigerator in well-sealed jugs. I dilute the syrup to some convenient volume with boiled water and use poly-seal caps on gallon wine jugs. When you're going to brew, get the jugs out of the fridge and let them come to room temperature. Invert sugar syrup makes malt extract seem easy to handle by comparison: when you first take it out of the fridge, you couldn't pour it out of the jug in much under four hours.

Malting grain. I haven't malted and I wasn't going to include this procedure at first. But since then, the food situation in the United States has deteriorated and I can foresee a time when malt extract may not be available or may cost so much as to make the work required to malt your own worth it. Further, more and more people (particularly those who may wind up buying this book) are getting into farming, at least on a small scale, or into buying food at the grain and feed, so that they have a source of grain ready at hand.

A little biochemistry will help you understand what's going on. The principal ingredient of grain is starch. The malting process converts the starch to sugar so that the yeast can ferment it to alcohol. Barley, as it sprouts, produces an enzyme, called amylase, which can split the starch into sugars. The first step in malting, then, is to cause seed barley to sprout.

If you're going to use barley that you haven't grown yourself, FIND OUT WHAT IT HAS BEEN TREATED WITH AND WHAT THAT WILL DO TO YOU before you buy. Other than that, try to make sure that the grain is fully ripened and has an even size.

Sprouting requires keeping the grain wet and between 63° and 86° F. until it starts. Begin by soaking in water warmed to the right temperature, changing the water every 24 hours. Soak it for two to six days. Drain the grain and spread it out on a wet surface of toweling or sacking. Keep the grain wet and in the temperature range until it sprouts and the sprouts grow to about a quarter of an inch long. This will take anywhere from one to two weeks. If the grain is more than one inch deep or is covered to keep in the heat, it must be turned twice a day to let air in.

Once you have the sprouts, the next step is to dry the grain out. You must use moderate heat, keeping it under 120° F. Problem: my oven's lowest marked temperature is 250° F. You may have to rig a special malting oven. Once the grain is dry, increase the temperature slightly, keeping it under 140° F., to toast the malt. Stop after 15 minutes if you want a pale malt, or wait until the color of the grain is what you want, if you want dark malt.

Extracting malt. This is the next step if you've malted your own grain, but you can also buy malted grain by mail-order and start here. Again, this is something I haven't tried, so all I can do is give you bare-bones directions.

More biochemistry: what you're going to do now is get the starch and the amylase out of the barley seeds and into a water solution where the enzyme can do its stuff. Like yeast, the enzyme requires a specific temperature range to work, but it's more picky.

First, crack four pounds of the malted grain. This can be done in a coffee grinder or with a rolling pin. Put two gallons of water into a plastic bucket and heat to 150° F. Your best bet for heating is a good thermometer and a 50-watt aquarium heater. Add the cracked malt, put a piece of plastic over the bucket and wrap it in a blanket to keep the heat in. You've got to keep the temperature between 145° and 150° for about eight hours while the starch is converted to sugar.

After about eight hours of mashing, as the process is called, test for residual starch. Take a small amount of the mash and add a little iodine. If the mess turns blue, starch is present and you'll have to keep on mashing. Throw your test sample away—iodine is poisonous. Once the mash passes the starch test, strain it into a pan, add two ounces of hops, and boil for forty-five minutes to an hour. Strain this and you're right where you would have been if you'd opened a can of malt extract and dissolved some in the wort.

The amounts in this procedure produce enough for five gallons of wort, a double batch of the basic recipe. This size is determined by the size of the mashing bucket and the 50-watt heater. If you want to produce larger amounts, keep things in proportion: e.g., eight pounds of malt, four gallons of water, and a 100-watt heater. Remember that your critical design factor is maintaining the 145° to 150° F. for as long as it takes for the starch to be converted.

Stretching yeast. Although I know of five different ways to stretch yeast, I still use a fresh package every time I brew. Every method of re-using yeast runs the risks of contamination by wild spores and of mutation or reversion by the yeast itself. Once the form of the yeast is changed, it can do things to your brew that you won't like. Since there may be off-setting advantages to stretching yeast, I've given you two simple and two complex methods and indicated my objections to them.

Simple method I: If you have a large batch—say thirty to fifty gallons—you can ferment it with a single package of yeast, even though the package is marked "adequate for five gallons." You do it by starting the yeast ahead of time and letting it multiply itself a few times before adding it to the wort.

You want enough starting solution to equal ten to fifteen percent of your wort (the usual rule of thumb is one pint of solution for every ten gallons of wort). The starting solution should have about the same specific gravity as your wort. You can use one-fourth cup of sugar per pint of solution as an approximation or you can work it out finer if you want.

Prepare the yeast following the instructions that come with it and add it and yeast nutrient to the sugar solution. When the sugar solution is fermenting along well, stir it up and add it to your freshly prepared wort. This is one method I can recommend.

Why not either make up the wort and then add the packet of yeast to 12.5 percent of it or just add the package to all of the wort and wait? You can do either of these things, but you're forced to leave the wort unprotected until it gets fermenting along.

Simple method II: Re-use the yeast sediment left at the bottom of the vat after fermenting one batch for the next batch. I'd recommend cooling your wort in the pan before adding it to the vat so as not to damage the yeast. In addition to the previous objections, I would add that you can get a lot of yeast on the bottom in time.

I've asked brewers who use this method how they know when to start new yeast. They say that when a batch develops an off-taste, it's time to change. OK, but by the time you discover the off-taste, you've probably brewed one or two additional batches. Saving a few dimes leaves you with two or three batches that don't taste the way you want them to. Worth it? Maybe not stretching over long periods of time, but I've done it for a batch or two with no harm.

Complex method I: With both complex methods, you culture yeast apart from the wort under sterile or nearly sterile conditions. Although sterile culturing avoids contamination, in time the yeast may mutate and revert. In the first method, you add a package of yeast to about three-fourths of a quart of fresh wort. This mixture is put into a sterilized bottle fitted with a fermentation lock to avoid contamination. When you're ready to start a batch of brew, add half the contents of the bottle to the wort, stir it up, and draw off enough new wort to replenish the bottle. Repeat the process for each new batch. There will come a time, however, when the yeast in the culture bottle will ferment the contents to the point where the alcohol will do them in. When you pour the starter into your waiting wort, nothing will happen and you'll know it's time to start over again. (If you haven't had some off-tastes tell you already.)

Complex method II: This method is a trifle more sterile than method I and tries to lengthen the time it takes for the culture bottle to brew itself into alcoholic stupor. It's also more trouble. Add the yeast to about three-fourths of a quart of sugar and water solution. Put the mixture into a sterilized bottle, fit a fermentation lock, and let it ferment for two days. Stir it and add half to the waiting wort. Replenish the bottle with new sugar solution, stopper the bottle, and put it in the fridge. (When I was using this method, I always began to wonder at this point whether the yeast would ferment enough CO_2 to break the bottle before the fridge cooled the yeast into dormancy. The fridge won the race every time.)

Two days before you're going to need yeast again, remove the bottle from the fridge, take the stopper out, put on the fermentation lock, and let it get started on its way.

There may be one other method worth recommending. If you're into microbiology and sterile transfer technique, you could take up yeast culture as a separate hobby. I suspect that it would cost you more to get set up than it does for brewing.

Summing up: In my opinion, a dime is very little to pay to avoid the risks and troubles of stretching. Occasionally, however, I get fascinated by yeast at work and find the grief involved in method II an acceptable price to pay for the entertainment of watching fermentation start up from nothing.

Fermenting and After

Driving fermentation. You will recall from the last chapter that a constant temperature is desirable and that fermentation takes place at a faster rate at a higher temperature. Seeking to bring about one or both of these conditions, some brewers hit on the idea of putting an aquarium heater in the vat and letting it heat the wort. Most of those who use a heater have shorter fermentation times in mind and tend to brew around 80° F.

If you want to try this method, the first step is to get a heater and a thermometer that you can put in your vat. I've used a 100-watt heater to drive 16-gallon batches at about 75°, checking temperatures with a stainless steel aquarium thermometer. The basic recipe, two and a half gallons, would probably need a 25-watt heater. The level of the wort must come up and cover the thermostat in the heater in order for the heater to maintain a constant temperature. You'll probably have to suspend the heater in some way so that the wort will be at the right level.

Make up the wort as usual, put it in the vat, turn on the heater, and let the wort come to the desired temperature before pitching the yeast. After the yeast has been pitched and the heavy fermentation is underway, foaming yeast will probably overwhelm the top of the heater and make it work erratically. Even if it doesn't work as well as it would in an aquarium, the heater still has enough going to do the job.

Determining when to bottle is something of a problem when you use this method. Your hydrometer is probably calibrated for 60° F., and even though you can use the correction tables in Appendix C, you may find yourself bottling early because more of the lighter alcohol rises to the top of the vat and gives a false reading. I bottled early the first time I used this method and cleaning up was a troublesome chore. To avoid problems, it's best to let fermentation go all the way and then prime the wort back (see *priming* in this section). You can determine when fermentation is complete by shining a flashlight on the surface of the wort and looking for bubbles rising to the surface. You want none (if you have the patience to wait) or damn few at most.

If a constant, rather than a higher temperature is your goal, the same procedure can be used. The catch is that the constant temperature must always be *higher* than the surrounding temperature. If you want a constant low temperature, you could put the vat in a refrigerator and drive it with a small heater. An old refrigerator, even with the motor shot, makes an excellent insulated box for your vat, whether you're trying to drive at high or low temperatures.

Fermenting anaerobically. This may sound fearsome and complicated, but it's quite simple. The idea is to ferment away from the outside air. The fermentation lock, widely used in winemaking and easily obtainable by mail-order, makes anaerobic fermentation possible. To use this procedure, you need to get three fermentation locks (for the ten quart batch), three one-gallon jugs—ESCHEW VINEGAR JUGS—some yeast energizer, and a turkey baster and test jar, if you don't have them already.

The basic procedures are followed until the brewing head goes down and then the wort continues anaerobically. Put the vat where it can be siphoned from. Make sure the jugs are clean and then put one-half teaspoon of yeast energizer in each of them. Siphon the wort from the vat into the jugs, leaving as much sediment as possible behind. Fit the locks on the jugs and let the fermentation continue until it's time to bottle. At that time, I siphon the wort from the jugs back into the vat, again leaving the sediment behind, and bottle from the vat. I could bottle directly from the jugs, but my way mixes the brew from all three jugs and seems a little easier.

There are a number of advantages to anaerobic fermentation, some practical and some theoretical. If you're looking to increase production without getting into bigger batches, this method frees the vat in about half the time. Also, since acetobacters can't function in an air-less environment, you don't have to worry about your brew turning to vinegar. As a consequence, you can use higher temperatures to increase the rate of fermentation. In fact, combining driving and anaerobic fermentation is a common technique.

In addition to avoiding the risk of vinegar, anaerobic fermentation makes the yeast do more of what we want. Without air, yeast spend more time making alcohol and less time building cell walls. Therefore, for a given amount of sugar in the wort, we should wind up with more clout and less sediment.

Priming. Priming is adding sugar to completely fermented wort so that the yeast will have something to ferment to condition the brew. There are a number of traditional amounts of sugar that are supposed to be enough to get flat wort back to where it should be. Oddly enough, most of them are correct. The one I learned as a child, a teaspoon of sugar per quart, will give a hydrometer reading of 1.003 to 1.004. This is a little flatter than our basic method, but it's still plenty of sparkle.

My conservative rule of thumb is one teaspoon per degree rise in specific gravity per gallon. Stating the rule this way makes it easy to calculate the amount of sugar needed both for flat wort (five degrees rise wanted) and wort that has only gone a little beyond the bottling point. The sugar should be dissolved in water since adding it directly to the wort causes too much foam and interferes with bottling. Use the smallest amount of water you can to dissolve the sugar, since the water lowers the hydrometer reading you're trying to raise. I've found that sugar will dissolve easily in about half its own volume of water with a little heating.

As an example, suppose you go away for the weekend and come back Sunday night to find that your ten-quart batch is now reading 1.002. You want to bottle now before you go to bed. You need a reading of 1.005, so you want to raise 2½ gallons (10 quarts), 1.005 minus 1.002, or three degrees. Therefore, you need 2½ × 3 = 7½ teaspoons of sugar.

If you're going to be priming flat wort only, you can make up a standard priming solution. I developed one while I was brewing 16 gallon batches. The recipe I had called for brewing the wort flat, adding two cups of sugar, and then bottling from the vat. I wanted to use a transfer pail and bottle in my kitchen, rather than in the cellar, where I kept the vat. I dissolved the two cups of sugar into enough water to make one quart (32 ounces) of solution. I then siphoned from the vat into the transfer pail, added two ounces of priming liquid for every gallon of wort in the pail, and then bottled from the pail in the kitchen. Very convenient.

The priming solution is less conservative than the rule of thumb—six teaspoons of sugar per gallon compared to five—but still within safe limits. If you like using the solution, you can make it up in quantity and store it in the fridge. Dissolve the sugar and then dilute so that you have twice the volume of solution as the sugar you started with. For example, if you start with four cups of sugar, you'll end up with two quarts of priming solution. If you want to experiment with condition, it's convenient to do it either by using more priming solution or by making up stronger solutions. I'd advise small increments, as always.

Whenever you're priming, double-check your arithmetic before you do anything and CHECK THE PRIMED WORT WITH A HYDROMETER when you're done. Any mistake causes grief. If you discover the mistake before you bottle, you can add sugar if you're low or let the wort ferment a little if you're high. If you discover it after you bottle, you'll need the section on *Saving mistakes* in this chapter.

Priming gives your brewing schedule flexibility, but it's important not to abuse your waiting wort. Remember that completely fermented wort has no blanket of CO_2 to protect it and is, therefore, vulnerable to all the ills wort is heir to. Further, after fermentation is completed, a layer of yeast can form on the surface of the wort. While harmless, this layer can impart a characteristic "yeast-bit" taste to your brew.

Jacking. Suppose you want a greatly higher percentage of alcohol in your drink (more smash to the slash). Adding more sugar to the wort won't hack it because past a certain point, about 14 percent, the alcohol kills the yeast. Distilling your finished brew would hack it, but getting and running a still is a lot of grief (everything has to be made of copper or glass; the still has to be tended constantly) and distilling really is illegal—people get put in jail for it every week. Jacking, the process by which apple cider becomes applejack, both hacks it and is legal.

The idea behind jacking is simple: brew is a mixture of water and alcohol. Get it cold enough but not too cold and the water will freeze but the alcohol won't. Pour off the alcohol (so how come anti-freeze works?). You can't expect to pour off pure 200-proof, but you do get a more highly alcoholic drink.

Because I'm not into hard liquor, I've never gone in for jacking on any large scale or with any consistency. In fact, I usually do it by accident. I come home, find no cold homebrew, try to speed the process by putting a bottle in the freezer, and then forget the bottle. By the time I remember, it's pretty slushy. I pour the liquid into my glass and put the bottle in the refrigerator to thaw. The first drink is usually pretty strong, but refills get weaker and weaker until I'm drinking water and give up. A pleasant way to drink.

If you want to be systematic about it, I'd recommend brewing your wort flat and aging it in gallon jugs, or bigger containers if you have them, to save work in bottling, siphoning, and capping. The original New England method of jacking is to put hard cider in an upright barrel during the fall and leave it out on the porch overnight. In the morning, the layer of ice that has formed on top during the night is skimmed before it can thaw. The process is continued until whoever's doing it is satisfied with what's left. Later in the fall, most of the barrel freezes, leaving a core of highly alcoholic liquid. This core is tapped and siphoned off.

If the weather's amenable, you could follow this process, but if it's not, you're going to have to adapt it to whatever source of cold you have. I'd say that you're going to be better off skimming ice than letting the whole thing freeze to slush and then pouring liquid off the slush. The ice is going to be nearly pure water and you can continue the process just by letting new ice form. The liquid that comes from slush is a mixture of alcohol and water and you never can tell how much to let melt. If you have a freezer or a big freezer section in your fridge, you might try plastic gallon ice-cream buckets. Whatever you use, make sure to leave enough room for expansion due to freezing.

Transporting homebrew. The layer of sediment at the bottom of the bottle keeps homebrew from being portable. Frost heaves and potholes in the roads shake my brew around so much even on a short drive that it looks like a bottle of milk when I get to where I'm going. I've tried to take bottles away and then see how long it takes them to settle down to where the brew can be poured off. Two weeks is a short time if my experience is typical.

I've come to appreciate this stick-in-the-mud attitude of homebrew. It won't let itself be hauled around to parties, where it would be given a cursory gulping as some sort of curiosity. You can share it only with people you like well enough to invite to your home. Homebrew.

There is a method of transporting, but it's comforting to know that it's less than perfect. It's a lot of trouble and the resulting brew is a distinct notch worse for the procedure. But, if you want to do it, put whatever brew you want to take, four or five clean empty bottles, and your glass pitcher in the fridge to get cool. When everything's chilled, open a bottle of brew and pour it into the pitcher using the same technique as when drinking. Pour the brew from the pitcher back into the chilled bottles. If you have a glass funnel, you could use it, but a plastic funnel will add to your problems since it causes the brew to foam.

The brew will foam some no matter how cold you get it, so pour it into a bottle until the foam reaches the top, then switch to another bottle. I usually get three or four bottles going at the same time and rinse and use the bottles that the brew started out in. As the foam subsides, pour more brew into the bottles. Depending on the condition of the brew and its temperature, it could take anywhere from three to six or more pourings to get a particular bottle filled. When all of the brew has been transferred, cap the filled bottles and rinse and store the excess empty bottles. Although the resulting brew will be flatter and will lose a little in flavor, it can be transported. Also, when you drink it, you can dispense with the careful pouring technique or even drink it right out of the bottle.

If you plan your drinking parties six weeks or more in advance, there is one good way to transport homebrew. Right after it's bottled, haul it to wherever you're going to be drinking it. The brew is already cloudy because fermentation hasn't been completed, so the jouncing around doesn't add to the problems. Store and age it just like you would at home. You have to be on good terms with the people who live where the drinking is going to take place. They've got custody of your fortune in bottles.

Saving Mistakes

Even the best brewer sometimes makes bad brew.

—German proverb

The first thing to do about mistakes is to get into the right mental frame. You're probably going to make a few, and recognizing that in advance lessens the shock when you do. Keep in mind that most mistakes can be rectified, at least in part, with only a slight loss in quality. And if all measures fail, you're out a dollar or so, cash, and whatever time you put into brewing (maybe an hour and a half). If you've been keeping good notes on what you've been doing, even these painful cases offer you a chance to find out what went wrong and thus gain in brewing knowledge.

Stuck fermentations are the most serious and the most common problem. The simplest cure is to add yeast nutrient and energizer and to stir up the wort to add air. If this fails to get things going again, prepare fresh yeast and add it. Try to keep your wort at an even temperature from now on.

If the fermentation sticks just before bottling and you can't get it going and your brew is *flat*, you can try making shandy. After I had a large batch of dark brew stick, I got the idea of adding carbonation by means of mixing the flat brew with sparkling soda pop. Patterning my solution after shandy, originally a mixture of beer and lemonade, I mixed the brew with a number of lemon-flavored soda pops. I found that Tom Collins mix did the best job, but this is obviously a matter of personal taste. The result was drunk with gusto by a large number of people, including some who had had shandy drinking experience. (You might try original shandy as a summertime drink.)

If you don't like the taste of shandy or can't go for the half-and-half dilution, you might take the flat brew and try *jacking*.

Exploding bottles are more upsetting than flat brew, but you have a better chance to save quality, although you may lose quantity. The most common (if not the only) cause of those muffled BLOUPS you hear coming from the cellar is bottling too soon. Having steeled your nerves for a messy job (try a frosty bottle of a more reliable brew), move the surviving bottles to the bathtub or someplace else that can be safely inundated by wildly foaming brew. Get your churchkey out and very gently lift up a little on the caps. Pry them off enough to let the gas come out.

If you caught it in time, a lot of gas will come spilling out and things will quiet down. Open a bottle and draw off enough brew for a hydrometer reading. If the brew is below 1.005, you can recap the batch and put it back downcellar, confident that you're not going to have to re-do the job a few days later. If the reading is still high, leave the bottles uncapped and let the brew ferment until you get a bottling reading.

If you didn't catch it in time, things are going to be a little more spectacular. Foam and liquid will come shooting out around the edge of the cap, giving it the appearance of an old-fashioned flying saucer trying to get off, but stuck. In very bad cases, you'll get fountain effects and lose about a third to a half of the brew, in addition to stirring up what remains until it looks like a bad storm at sea. Let it have its way (you don't have any choice), take a hydrometer reading to see if you're down to where you can re-cap, and if so, consolidate your bottles so that you get the level of the brew up in the necks of the ones remaining.

Clean up the tub and hope for the best.

It's much easier to deal with brew that ferments correctly but *doesn't taste the way you want or expect*. Often the strangeness of the taste will be temporary and extra aging will fix it. I've already mentioned my early batch made with brown sugar. After four weeks of aging, it still had a taste that made me think more about pouring it on pancakes than drinking it straight. I decided to dump it, but since I had lots of empties on hand, I let it stay in the bottles until I needed them. After another four months, I tried a bottle and found it quite good. I had a similar experience with a batch made using "instant" hops. This case took almost six months.

Sometimes the taste isn't bad but is so unexpected that you may have trouble in drinking the brew. My first two batches came out flat and tasting more like apple cider than the commercial beer I'd been expecting. Fresh cider was available at the time so I bought some and mixed it with the brew. After a little experimentation, I discovered that two parts brew to one part fresh cider made a drink that was both palatable and potent.

Sometimes you may come to like what was at first unexpected. Some people like the cidery-tasting brew best and I like it occasionally. Now and then I make a batch on purpose.

If you've been getting *cidery taste,* by the way, and you want to avoid it, I would advise heavier body, adding hops, and using either a high temperature and a fast fermentation or the anaerobic fermentation technique using energizer. The cidery taste is rather common, but not necessary, to beginning homebrew.

Expanding Your Repertoire

Handling bigger batches. When I began brewing, I started with the ten-quart batch size and stayed with it for about a year. The small frequent batches gave me a good chance to experiment, and after I'd added anaerobic fermentation, I fell into an easy weekly routine. Every Saturday, I'd transfer a batch from the vat to the jugs, bottle the batch that had been in anaerobic fermentation and was ready, and then make up a new batch to go into the vat. The whole process took a little less than an hour and yielded a steady supply of ten quarts of brew a week—more than adequate to my needs. When summer rolled around, I began to have ideas about giving parties and decided the time had come to put my large vat to use.

If you've been brewing in small batches and you want to move to bigger ones, it's fairly easy. About the only piece of new gear you'll need is a larger vat. The procedures will be slightly different and you may find it easier to start from a different recipe, rather than multiplying your good small batch one. When I went to larger batches, I began with an eight-gallon recipe given to me by a friend, who got it from a college friend, who got it from an old blacksmith in Ohio.

Old Ohio Blacksmith Brew

> 1 five-pound bag of sugar
>
> 1 teaspoon salt
>
> 1 teaspoon gypsum
>
> 1 teaspoon citric acid
>
> 2 to 4 ounces of hops
>
> 1 three-pound can of malt extract
>
> 2 teaspoons yeast nutrient
>
>   yeast

Making up is done piecemeal and starts like the Momma's-gonna-have-a-baby scene in the movies of the forties: Papa's in the kitchen boiling water like mad. I first get the water for the hop tea going, then put on my teakettle. Every time the kettle whistles, I use the hot water, refill the kettle, and put it back on the stove. Like Doc says, "You can't have too much boiling water."

I put my small vat—the three-gallon bucket—in the kitchen sink and put the sugar, salt, gypsum (if I have some around), and the citric acid in it. When the teakettle whistles, I pour the water onto the dry ingredients and stir to dissolve with a long-handled wooden spoon. Sometimes I wait for another kettle of boiling water and sometimes I just add enough cold tap water to finish the job.

When the water for the hops comes to a boil, I put in the hops and carry out the whole procedure. While the hops are simmering, I carry the bucket down to the cellar and empty it into the big vat. When the hop tea is ready, I pour it into the bucket and haul it down, refilling the pan before I go so that I can dissolve the malt. Once the malt is dissolved—using boiling water from the kettle can save time—it goes into the bucket and down to the big vat. I then use the garden hose to fill the vat to the desired volume and let the wort come to room temperature before I add the nutrient and pitch the yeast.

The wort is fermented flat—I usually drive it with an aquarium heater—and then primed for bottling. I prime for two reasons. First, getting an accurate hydrometer reading to bottle is difficult. The wort is around 75° F. instead of 60° and the alcohol and the lighter, more fermented portion of the wort comes to the top. Even after I make temperature corrections (see chapter VII), the reading is lower than it should be because of the lower density of the alcohol and the partially fermented wort. I wind up bottling too soon—much grief. Second, bottling five cases, a double batch, is a big job. I like to be able to choose when to do it—within limits.

When it's time to bottle, I use two buckets (they balance) to transfer the wort from the vat in the basement back to the kitchen, where I set up for bottling. Conditioning and aging are the same as for small batches.

The chief advantage of big batches is convenience. Not only do you make a lot at once and avoid several making up and cleaning up operations, you can also manipulate the recipe to avoid unpleasant tasks like measuring malt extract. My standard big batch, sixteen gallons, began by doubling the recipe. Later, I decided I'd like a heavier-bodied brew, but rather than getting too precise, I made adjustments by the can of extract and the bag of sugar. My present favorite brew uses three cans of dark malt extract, two bags of sugar, and eight ounces of hops. Everything else is just doubled. When I've finished making up, there is no extra malt to put to harden in the fridge, no hops to rewrap in aluminum foil, and no spare sugar to keep from the ants.

Making soft drinks. In theory, at least, soft drinks are more dangerous to make in the home than good, honest, alcoholic homebrew. If you compare soft drink recipes and procedures with those for homebrew, you'll see the danger at once. The ingredients for both are nearly the same: flavorings, sugar, water, and yeast. When we brew, we allow very nearly all of the sugar to ferment to alcohol before we bottle. We bottle, the last bit of sugar ferments, the yeast stops, and the brew begins to age and clear. But with the soft drinks, we add the yeast, get things going, and bottle *immediately.* Ye gods! All of the sugar is still there, unfermented, ready to turn to huge volumes of gas. If and when it does, your bottles blow up.

When I turned my hand to soft drinks, I had never yet had a bottle of brew blow—despite dire warnings to the contrary. My first attempts at homebrewed lemon and ginger beer, however, produced a number of broken bottles, a number of syrupy messes, some truly spectacular foam fountains, and some badly shaken nerves. I retreated to root beer extract.

Dangers aside, you already have all the gear you need to make soft drinks, and since making them can also be fun and cheap, you should at least consider them—particularly if you have non-drinkers in the house. You can work them into your brewing schedule any number of ways, but keep in mind that they're ready to drink after about a week in the bottle and that they don't improve with age—just get more yeasty and testy.

I usually use my small vat to mix in, and make the batch up right after I rinse the vat after bottling the brew. Once the soft drinks are bottled, I rinse out the vat again and use it to make up a batch of brew. This way I bottle and cap everything at once.

Root beer extract is the simplest thing to start with. You can pick from several brands at most grocery stores. Each brand comes complete with instructions, but no two sets of instructions that I've ever seen are the same. Perhaps the best thing to do at first is to try all of the brands, following their own instructions, and then pick the brand you like best for further experimentation.

Next in ease and safety are the various preparations that you'll find advertised in the mail-order catalogs. The two chief ones are ginger beer and sarsaparilla. Ginger beer is like ginger ale, but has a stronger flavor. Sarsaparilla is for licorice freaks. (Hoppy could have stayed out of a lot of fist fights if he'd only have had some licorice sticks made up to look like cigars and layed off ordering sarsaparilla in redneck barrooms.) The preparations come with instructions, but they're sometimes incomprehensible. If you've made root beer from extract, apply what you know, use common sense, and everything will turn out OK.

Finally, you can be adventurous and strike out on your own (double-edged, that phrase). I'm going to give you some general directions, but I've got to warn you that you're headed into dangerous territory. Let's say that you're going to make up a two and a half gallon batch. First, get some flavoring. Five lemons cut into slices might do for a first try. Add sugar, about four to five cups for the two and a half gallons. You can add whatever spices you think might do the drink some good. I can't guide you here, but I can warn you that ginger speeds up the action of yeast, so if you use it, look out. Next, add water. If you want to get the most out of your fruit, you might heat the water. This can, however, cause a haze and can add a bitter taste in the case of lemon. (A bitter taste might be what you want if you're planning to use the soft drink as a mixer.)

Stir to dissolve, let the mixture come to room temperature, and add yeast. The kind of yeast isn't critical. Since it will ferment only a little, it doesn't have to be alcohol-tolerant, and since it remains in suspension, it never gets a chance to form a firm sediment on the bottom of the bottle. As to amount, I advise starting with one quarter of a teaspoon, softening it in warm water as in brewing, and then stirring it in. You can then bottle immediately or let the drink ferment from twelve to twenty-four hours and then bottle.

And now let me give you the fruit of bitter experience. You're going to have to watch this stuff like a hawk. Put the bottles in the place you use for conditioning and let it sit for a few days—more in cold weather, less in hot. After a couple of days, take a bottle out and carry it to the kitchen sink (use the bathtub later on). Open the bottle. If it's still flat, note how much fizz it does have, recap, and put that bottle back in the case. Estimate how much more time will be required to condition the drink, cut your estimate drastically, and at the end of the drastically cut period of time, get another bottle out and test it.

When you find a bottle that seems to fizz adequately when you open it, recap it, and put it in the fridge to cool. Try it again when the drink is chilled—it may not have enough fizz then. Keep trying until you have the right amount of fizz. When you do, PUT THE WHOLE LOT IN THE FRIDGE and drink it up.

In this fashion, through vigilance you remain free from explosions and live as happily as one can who messes with homemade soft drinks.

Hardening cider. Making hard cider is only slightly more trouble than making homebrew. You do have a much greater chance of winding up with vinegar, however, so it is a very good idea to ferment anaerobically. If you want to harden cider, you've first got to get unhardened cider *to which no preservatives have been added.* This may be bothersome in some parts of the country, but in Connecticut most of the large orchards press their own cider and sell it right from the press every fall.

When you get your cider home, take a hydrometer reading to see how much sugar it contains. The amount varies from year to year and depends on the length of the growing season, the amount of sunshine and rain, and all those other things that winegrowers talk about all the time. When you have your reading, go to the section on priming and add enough sugar (dissolved in water) to put the hydrometer reading between 1.060 and 1.070.

Adding sugar to natural cider may make the pure blanch, and if you're that pure, better bail out right now.

Now that they're gone, I'll hip you to the next ghastly step. The cider contains natural yeasts and would harden by itself if left alone. However, it has been my experience (and that of orchard owners around here) that the cider contains many bad acetobacters. You get the picture: the natural yeast turns the natural cider to natural hard cider and the natural acetobacters turn the natural hard cider to natural cider vinegar. What's needed is a little artifice.

Theoretically, there are a number of ways to defeat the foe. First, you can harden the cider untreated at a lowish temperature and hope for the best. I've tried at around 60° F. and still wound up with vinegar. Next, you can slap the whole thing untreated under a fermentation lock. OK, but I've had people tell me that the natural yeast won't start the process under anaerobic conditions. You can add yeast and put the whole thing under a fermentation lock. This is the procedure recommended by local orchardists. Finally, since you are going to add yeast, anyway, you can take the process to its logical conclusion and get rid of the acetobacters before you start. This method is used by careful winemakers and I've tried it myself with good results.

To do it, for each gallon of cider, dissolve one campden tablet (or an eighth of a teaspoon of sodium metabisulphite) in a little water and stir it into the cider. Let the cider stand for about twenty-four hours to give the sulpher dioxide that will be generated a chance to get the acetobacters (and, let's face it squarely, the natural yeasts) and dissipate from the cider. Once everything is gone, pitch new yeast and ferment the cider under a fermentation lock.

Let the cider finish fermenting and clear itself before you try to bottle it. I've bottled at 1.005, thinking to have nice, sparkling cider. No dice. The apple solids, yeast, and other stuff are all in suspension and fall out on the bottle bottom. If it were yeast alone, it would form a nice layer and I could pour the sparkling cider off of it with a certain amount of care. But the apple solids form a thick, loose cloud on the bottom that starts moving at the slightest pretext. I'd be lucky to get even half of the bottle poured before the cloud hits the pitcher. And the stuff tastes bad. If you want sparkling cider, let it finish fermenting, siphon it away from all the muck, prime it to 1.005, and then bottle it.

Opinions on aging cider vary. I harden the earliest cider I can get and drink it for Thanksgiving and Christmas. Some say that cider starts to go downhill after six months in the bottle. Others, however, maintain that spring is the earliest you should drink your fall cider. I don't know, but I'm waiting for the time when I can put up a giant batch and drink a bottle every week or so while keeping careful notes.

Making wine. Once you've learned the basic brewing skills, you will know most of what you need to make wine. As far as additions to your kit go, winemaking requires gear for handling fruit (or whatever you're going to ferment), wine bottles and something to seal them—usually corks (although you could use beer bottles and caps)—and equipment for fermenting anaerobically—fermentation locks, casks, etc.

I haven't made wine on my own for two reasons. First, I have a friend who does. By helping him every year, I learned how to do it without having to foot the bills or shoulder the responsibility. Second, the nomadic life I've been leading hasn't been stable enough to warrant wine. Brewing requires little equipment and takes little time until I can drink what I've made. When I make mistakes, they don't cost much money, and if I hustle a little, they don't even cause me to run dry. When I have to move, I can easily pack the essential gear, invite all my friends to one farewell blast where we drink up all the current production, then turn the bottles in for the deposit.

Winemaking would take some heavy equipment (or a lot of work to do without it), and at least six months to a year of aging to improve the wine to where it would repay the work. If you're making wine from grapes, you make it all at once, which requires money all at once and concentrates risk. Losing even five cases of brew sets me back about six bucks. Losing a thirty-gallon cask of wine, like my friend did one year, could cost around sixty. I know it would be foolish to try to move fifty gallons of wine 2,500 miles, even if it were packed in casks instead of gallon jugs and quart bottles. And I suspect it would be foolish to try to drink that much up in a day—maybe even more so, if I invited both friends and enemies to help the work along.

But if and when I do settle down, I fully intend to get into winemaking, and if you're pretty well settled, I recommend it to you. You can start in small batches, you can avoid the need to process fruit in various ways—concentrates, for example—and you can drink it green. Best of all, you'll probably be able to find help locally and there are many good books on beginning winemaking. If you're interested in making wine scientifically from grapes, get a copy of Walter S. Taylor and Richard P. Vine, *Home Winemaker's Handbook* (Award Books). The authors make wine in New York State and the book has an abundance of information on wine, winemaking, and growing grapes. If you're interested in making wine from berries, cherries, rhubarb, fruit, potatoes, tomatoes, pimentos—in short, from everything *but* grapes—try C.J.J. Berry, *First Steps in Winemaking.* He's British and the British seem to have a thing about grapes.

(Yes, Vine and Berry are their real names.)

Making vinegar (on purpose) and other rare recipes. Take a look at the label on a can of Blue Ribbon Malt Extract and you'll see an offer for a free recipe booklet. If you don't have a can on hand, just write to:

Premier Malt Products, Inc.

1137 North 8th Street

Milwaukee, WS 53201

and ask for "Tested Recipes with Blue Ribbon Malt Extract." You'll receive a twenty-page booklet stuffed with legal things to do with malt extract.

The next time your grocer rings up your bags of sugar and cans of malt, gives you a superior look, and says, "Making booze, huh," you can stare him dead in the eye and proudly reply, "Nope. Chocolate malted pudding and homemade vinegar."

CHAPTER VI

Cooking With Brew

Do you look for ale and cakes here, you rude rascals?
— Henry VIII, V, iv

Ale Cake

2 cups brown sugar
1 cup shortening
2 eggs
1 cup chopped nuts
2 cups chopped dates
1 teaspoon cinnamon
½ teaspoon allspice
½ teaspoon ground cloves
3 cups sifted all-purpose flour
2 teaspoons baking soda
½ teaspoon salt
2 cups brew (or ale)

Cream sugar and shortening. Stir in eggs, nuts, dates, and spices. In a separate bowl, sift together flour, baking soda, and salt; stir in brew. Combine brew mixture with creamed mixture and mix until well blended. Bake in large tube pan in moderate oven (360° F.) 1 hour and 15 minutes or until cake tester or toothpick comes out clean when inserted in the cake. If desired, top with whipped cream, or a caramel icing.

Homebrew is so cheap that it can almost be considered a con-diment—like salt—to be used for whatever task comes to hand. Since I started brewing, I've been collecting and trying various recipes and I'd like to give you the benefit of my experience, even though it is limited.

The general organization of this chapter follows the idea of substituting homebrew for increasingly dissimilar fluids. The logical starting place, then, is to substitute

Brew for Beer

I begin with two or three recipes that may be something of a surprise, even to those familiar with cooking with beer.

Sewfflé. While suffering a recent period of brokeness, I got an idea of how to invite people to supper without getting broker and still have something to eat that wouldn't remind the guests, who were broke also, of the grim times. Homebrew, of course, served in wineglasses, and since I could then buy checked eggs at two and a half dozen for fifty cents, soufflés.

I'd heard that soufflés were tricky devils, prone to sinking to nothing in the oven and just not cooking at all, so I collected every conceivable soufflé recipe I could find. I had the Straightforward Soufflé, made with nothing but scratch ingredients; the various Short-cut Soufflés, plugging whatever ingredient cut the corner; and, clip-ped from a newspaper long ago, a soufflé using beer. I ate soufflés for a week, making each one up from a different recipe. I'm happy to report that the beer version, improved, of course, by homebrew, was genuinely easier and better than any of the others. Here it is:

12 ounces brew

1/3 cup diced onions

1/3 cup sliced scallion greens

1/4 teaspoon salt

6 eggs, separated

6 tablespoons all-purpose flour

1/2 teaspoon cornstarch

1/4 teaspoon sugar

dash of cayenne

6 tablespoons softened butter

Two tips on separating eggs: first, since the yolk has a great deal of fat, eggs are much easier to separate when cold. Second, any bit of yolk in the whites keeps them from beating up. Fish any yolk out with a piece of eggshell. Once the eggs are separated, bring everything to room temperature. Put the brew in a large saucepan and add the onions, scallion greens, and salt. Bring this to a boil and cook the onions until they're tender—it should take about five minutes.

In a separate bowl beat the egg yolks until they're creamy. Mix the flour, cornstarch, sugar, and cayenne and gradually beat this into the egg yolks. Then add the softened butter and beat the mixture until it's smooth and has the consistency of thick paste.

Take the brew and onions off the heat and let them cool slightly. Then add half of the brew to the yolk mixture, stirring to keep it smooth. Now pour the brew-yolks stuff back into the rest of the brew, stirring that. Bring the whole shebang to a boil, stirring constantly. It's going to look like thick custard, because that's what it more or less is.

Beat the egg whites until they're stiff but not dry and then fold them slowly into the beer-yolk mixture until they're thoroughly mixed. Get a 1½ quart oven dish—any casserole dish is OK—butter its bottom and sides and dust with flour. Pour the sewfflé mixture into the baking dish until it's an inch from the top. Bake in a preheated oven at 400° F. for a half hour. Serve immediately.

The advantages of the sewfflé over the soufflé are many. The procedure is simpler to start with and lends itself to more flexible cooking. Once the brew-yolk mixture has been prepared, it can be stored in the refrigerator. When you're ready to continue, take it out, reheat it to the boiling point, and get on with the egg white business. Also, it's all right to look in the oven while the sewfflé is cooking; it won't come a cropper as regular souffles are prone to do under the same conditions.

When you're ready to experiment, reduce the onions and scallions by half and make up the difference with ⅓ cup of whatever you think will go well with the flavor of the particular brew you intend to use. How about cheddar or Parmesan cheese, chopped herring, tuna, anchovies, ham, or tomatoes, or eggplant, or . . . ?

Better batters. Due to a sudden influx of fondue pots one Christmas, we found ourselves frequently cooking vegetables and pieces of meat in hot oil. We discovered that dipping mushrooms and shrimp in a batter before cooking them in the oil was a nice variation. Since that Christmas, I've discovered two batters based on beer, one very simple and the other rather complex.

Simple Batter

12 ounces brew
1 cup sifted all-purpose flour
1 tablespoon salt
1 tablespoon paprika

Pour the brew into a pan and sift the other ingredients into it, stirring with a wire whisk. As you use the batter, keep it whisked.

Italian Batter

10 ounces brew
1⅓ cups sifted all-purpose flour
2 tablespoons grated Parmesan cheese
1 tablespoon snipped parsley
1 teaspoon salt
 dash garlic powder
1 tablespoon olive oil
2 beaten egg yolks
2 stiff-beaten egg whites

Let the brew get flat. In a mixing bowl, combine flour, Parmesan, parsley, salt, and garlic powder. Stir in olive oil, egg yolks, and the flat beer; beat until smooth. Fold in stiff-beaten egg whites. Makes 3 cups.

If you want to substitute brew for beer in orthodox recipes, get a copy of *The Beer Cookbook* by Berneita Tolson and Edith McCaig (Belmont-Tower Books) and go from there. These women live in Great Falls, Montana, and cook like it. There's a good chapter on game and wildfowl, including serious recipes for bear, elk, and moose. The recipes that follow don't come from the book but from other sources—chiefly friends and newspapers. Some are unusual and some are classics. *The* classic:

Hot dogs steamed in brew. Wash the best hot dogs you can get and put them in whatever you use to simmer. Cover well with homebrew, bring to a boil, and simmer. How long to simmer is a matter of dispute; you'll hear recommendations of everywhere from five minutes to an hour. My guess is that the better the hot dogs are to begin with, the less you'll want to simmer. There's no disputing the fact that these are great with sauerkraut. In the rare chance that any are left over, slice them, brown the slices in butter, and scramble them with your breakfast eggs.

Norma's Stew. Norma, a roommate of some of the people in my first brewing class, came by this recipe somewhere in Germany, Australia, or the U.S. It's traditional, but you have to pick your tradition.

Chop up about one pound of onions. Cover the bottom of a pan with cooking oil and sauté the onions until glazed. They'll be transparent but not brown. If you want, you can add two small grated carrots. Put in two pounds of cut up beef. (Norma says it's better to buy chuck steak and cut it up yourself rather than to buy stewing beef.) Spices: salt, pepper, bay leaf, thyme, bouillon cubes or powder; everything to taste. Braise the beef on all sides until it gets to be sort of whitish-gray. Add a generous tablespoon of flour, mix it in, and cook it. You may have to add more oil.

Next add one to one and a half pints of homebrew that you've let come to room temperature. Stir well and make sure everything gets dissolved. Let it come to a boil, turn down, and simmer for at least an hour. If you don't want to simmer, you can put the whole thing in the oven, 250° to 300° F., for about three hours.

Serve it over rice or very thin egg noodles (the ones that look like yarn), butter, and parsley. *Wonderbar. Fair dinkum. Ace.*

Chicken in Brew

> 1 frying chicken, disjointed
> 4 tablespoons butter or margarine
> 16 small white onions, peeled or canned
> 1½ teaspoons salt
> 1½ teaspoons paprika
> few grains pepper
> ¼ teaspoon thyme
> ¾ cup brew
> ¼ cup tomato sauce
> 1 bay leaf
> ¼ cup heavy cream

Brown chicken pieces in butter; add onions; brown slightly. Add remaining ingredients except cream; bring to boil. Cover; simmer 30 minutes. Chill until fat rises to surface; skim off. Stir in cream; reheat. Makes 4 servings. I like to cook a little rice to go with the sauce.

Pilgrim Syrup

> 1 cup of brew
>
> 1 cup brown sugar

Heat brew, add sugar, and cook until the mixture turns to syrup—about 15 minutes. Serve it hot or cold like syrup. I wish I'd known about this recipe back when I had the brown sugar brew that I didn't like.

The Pilgrims had their hangups, but booze wasn't one of them. They brewed and later made rum.

Brew for Wine

Brew can be substituted in most traditional dishes calling for wine. Tolson and McCaig suggest adding "a small amount of sugar as an equalizer." Once you've decided to substitute brew, you might give some thought to changing other ingredients to suit. Traditional cheese fondue is made with Swiss cheese and white wine—an excellent combination. Think about dark homebrew and you'll go on to. . .

Cheddar Brew Fondew

> 1 pound aged natural Cheddar cheese
>
> 12 ounces brew
>
> 2 teaspoons dry mustard
>
> 1 teaspoon Worcestershire sauce
>
> 1 teaspoon paprika
>
> 1 teaspoon butter
>
> apple chunks
>
> bread chunks

Cheese fondues are tricky, so it pays to take a little extra care. Let the brew come to room temperature, pour it, and let it stand for at least an hour. You want it pretty flat. Grate the cheese. Mix the seasonings with one another. Melt the butter in the fondue pot and make sure the bottom is coated. Add the cheese a little at a time, stirring with a wooden spoon until the bit you've just added melts. Gradually add a cup of the brew, stirring constantly. Stir in the mixed seasoning and continue to stir the fondue until the mixture gets thick and moves with the spoon. If the cheese starts to get too thick, add more brew. Dunk in apple chunks and bread.

Brew for Water

A complete substitution would be carrying things too far, but . . .

Consider the bread recipe in chapter II. You could omit part or all of the water and use homebrew instead. I've found a recipe called *Sour French Bread*, that does essentially that. The only other change is that you'll need two packs of yeast instead of one. I guess the baking yeast can't take all that alcohol and need some help.

Free-style Skillet. In writing this chapter, I've learned an important thing: don't be bullied by a recipe. In comparing recipes for the "same" thing, I've found a lot of differences and finding them prompted me to make some differences of my own. It started small, but it's got to the point where I look at something like this:

Onion-Noodleburger Skillet

> 1 pound ground beef
> 1 medium onion, chopped
> 1 can onion soup
> 1 soup can water
> 3 cups uncooked fine egg noodles
> ¼ cup chili sauce

In skillet, brown beef and cook onion until tender. Stir to separate meat; pour off fat. Add remaining ingredients; bring to boil. Cover; cook over low heat 5 minutes or until noodles are done. Stir occasionally.

and do this:

One night I had half a pound of ground beef thawed out and knew I'd better get it cooked and eaten. Since I was working on a rewrite of this chapter, I wanted to use some homebrew if possible. I didn't have any fine egg noodles, but I did have some macaroni shells. I didn't think they could cook in the skillet so I started some water to boil so that they could go in cooked. I pulled an onion out of the sack and chopped it.

I browned the beef and onions, and then added a few pinches of sesame seed, since I had a lot left over from making granola. Since I was also cutting the recipe in half, I figured one soup can of brew, ten ounces, would do for the liquid and poured it on. I added the cooked shells (I used 1½ cups uncooked), stirred all, and simmered for awhile. I didn't have any chili sauce, so I left it out. Next time I'm going to add a dash or so of Worcestershire sauce for seasoning. But it was good without it.

Brewers' Popcorn

Once, after imbibing about one quart of a very hardy dark brew, I wanted to make something crunchy that would stand up to it. It was Sunday (which means that everything in the State of Connecticut was closed) and all I had on hand was some unpopped popcorn. The bland buttered version didn't seem strong enough and the sticky, molasses, crackerjacks kind was even more wrong. However, since there was nothing else on hand, I started popping the corn and thinking.

I melted some butter in a tin measuring cup. And then an idea came: I took down the Worcestershire sauce and put a few dollops into the melted butter (I half-remembered doing this sort of thing before and using it to anoint hamburger patties). When the corn was popped, I poured in the butter and mixed it up. While looking for the salt, I got into a strange chain of association. The Worcestershire sauce got me to thinking about Bloody Marys, Bloody Marys about tomato juice, and tomato juice about garlic salt, which is what I like to put in tomato juice. I found the garlic salt and sprinkled it on the popcorn liberally.

And the chain of association picked up an unexpected link. The tomato and the garlic got me to thinking Italian and a search of the fridge uncovered a box of grated Parmesan and Romano cheese. I shook in a stiff jolt and mixed that in. Unlike so many spur-of-the-moment inventions, this one worked and I recommend it to you for eating with homebrew.

CHAPTER VII

Advanced Drinking

The sway of alcohol over mankind is unquestionably due to its power to stimulate the mystical faculties of human nature, usually crushed to earth by the cold facts and dry criticisms of the sober hour. Sobriety diminishes, discriminates, and says no; drunkenness expands, unites, and says yes. It is in fact the great exciter of the Yes function in man. It brings its votary from the chill periphery of things to the radiant core. It makes him for the moment one with truth. Not through mere perversity do men run after it. To the poor and the unlettered it stands in the place of symphony concerts and of literature; and it is part of the deeper mystery and tragedy of life that whiffs and gleams of something that we immediately recognize as excellent should be vouchsafed to so many of us only in the fleeting earlier phases of what in its totality is so degrading a poisoning.

—William James

Using Alcohol

The long-established, orthodox view of alcohol use in America is axiomatically simple: except as anti-freeze or for sterilizing surgical instruments, alcohol has no *use*. All drinking is *abuse*. The first drop that enters the blood stream is seen as the scout of an invading army that will soon overwhelm the drinker and make him drunk in the short run and unhealthy, or dead, or damned in the long.

Recently this view has been challenged by scientific study. Although the damage that abuse does to health remains established, alcohol itself has been cleared of blanket charges of being a poison, harmful no matter how used. In fact, studies show that, other things equal, moderate drinkers actually live *longer* on the average than total abstainers (Second Special Report to the U.S. Congress on Alcohol and Health, 1974).

"Moderate" means a total of one and a half ounces of pure alcohol per day (three ounces of 100-proof whiskey or two pints of 4.8 percent beer), diluted and taken with meals. This amount had repeatedly been proposed as healthful (or, at least, not harmful) for over one hundred years without ever being taken seriously.

What about the orthodox view of drinking in the short run, that the impairment so obvious at high concentrations begins with the first drop. Again, studies have shown that this view is false. So far as the brain is concerned, alcohol works in two different ways. At low concentrations, it stimulates and enhances some functions, but, as the concentration increases, these functions return to "normal" levels and are then depressed.

One study showed, for example, that after drinking the equivalent of one ounce of pure alcohol (blood concentrations in the neighborhood of .04 percent), subjects could solve problems in symbolic logic *better* than they could stone cold sober. After two ounces, their performance was about the same as sober and did not deteriorate until they had had three ounces. I've found that I can read about 20 percent faster (particularly for my Ph.D. classes) when I put an ounce of rum in my coffee and that I can type the final draft of this book much faster and with fewer errors if I keep a glass of homebrew handy. (In fact, I'm going to pause to wet my whistle right now.)

The low concentration trip can be taken with any form of alcohol, but the natural conditioning of homebrew gives it a slight edge over everything but the very best champagne. Carbon dioxide in an alcoholic beverage enables the alcohol to get into the blood stream more rapidly by passing through the stomach wall directly. The more finely dissolved the carbon dioxide, the greater the effect. Thus, the alcohol in homebrew gets into the blood stream in a shorter period of time and we can get a higher and more precisely controlled concentration with less total alcohol.

Further, carbon dioxide may itself produce changes in consciousness. Not too much is known about it, but inhaling the gas has been used as a tool in psychotherapy, and as eminent an authority as Aldous Huxley says that some yoga breathing exercises increase the concentration of carbon dioxide in the blood stream to bring about a CO_2 high. (When you were a little kid, did anyone ever tell you that you could get "drunk" on aspirin and Coca-Cola? Did you ever try?) Again, the more finely dissolved the carbon dioxide is in the beverage, the faster it will get into the blood stream and the higher its concentration will be.

Drinking homebrew, then, especially in small amounts, can be very different from just plain drinking and from just plain drunk. First, the effect of homebrew is almost immediate. Most people drinking it for the first time notice that something has definitely happened before they finish the first small glass.

Second, the effect of homebrew seems always to be to cheer and exhilarate. In six years of homebrew drinking (including considerable excess at times), I've never seen homebrew make anyone irritable, pugnacious, or angry. In every case, it either continues a good mood or changes a sad and sober condition to a much better one. I hesitate to say that this will always be the case for everyone, but I hope so.

Finally, and most important, after small amounts of homebrew, one may have periods of up to six hours of those "fleeting earlier phases" that James writes about, at "the radiant core," "one with truth." As poetic as James's statement may seem, it is accurate, but, perhaps, incomplete. Doubtless the mystical faculties are stimulated, but, at the same time, the faculties attributed to sobriety—discrimination and discernment—may also be stimulated. Not only are opposites reconciled, but that which appeared to be homogenized and monolithic may be seen as diverse and varied.

Less is more.

Abusing Alcohol

Except for sex, the most well-known, well-documented, and popular human process must be abusing alcohol. Doing it is easy: we take one drink, then we feel like drinking more, then we drink more, and we end by drinking more than we intended (or needed). If we look at the physiology of the process, we can see that overdrinking is, in a sense, natural. Alcohol dehydrates body tissues. Therefore, after drinking, we feel thirsty and continued drinking makes us thirstier yet. Further, alcohol takes time to get out of the stomach and into the blood stream, but is metabolized as soon as it gets out. Thus, if some time has passed since we had an earlier drink, we grow more sober as we drink our current drink. Therefore, we tend to underestimate the power and eventual effect of what we're drinking.

Drunkenness is conventionally correlated to the concentration of alcohol in the blood. This concentration can be measured in a blood sample and can be easily estimated. Since one ounce of pure alcohol causes alcohol concentration to rise .04 percent (for an average body—about 150 pounds) and since an average body metabolizes one half ounce of alcohol per hour, if we know the concentration at any given time, the concentration later will be the same, plus the intake in ounces multiplied by .04 minus the difference in time in hours multiplied by .02. Or:

$$C_t = C_0 + .041 - .02t$$

This assumes immediate absorption which, as we have seen, is not the case, but, if a body has been drinking at a nice, steady rate for a longish period of time, the estimate is fairly close.

Conventionally, then, at a concentration of:

• 0.1 percent, you're showing some effects and are legally drunk in some states;

• 0.15 percent, you're legally drunk in most states;

• 0.3 percent, everyone can tell you're drunk;

• 0.4 percent, you'll pass out (and, in the old Western movies, Doc, played by John Carradine, who is at about 0.3 percent himself, digs the bullets out of your body);

• somewhere between 0.5 percent and 1 percent, you'll stop moving either your heart or your lungs and you'll die. What keeps more people from OD-ing on alcohol is that they can't keep drinking once they've passed out. But, if they manage to pass out with a large load still in the stomach waiting to get into the blood stream, it can be adios.

Given the risks, why should anyone wish to abuse alcohol? No universally satisfying answer can be given. The usual notion of a deathwish (let alone suppressed deathwish) runs counter to experience. Even abuse, as William James notes, has something of the YES about it, and working out a deathwish has got to be The Final NO. Maybe Blake comes closest: "The Road of Excess leads to the Palace of Wisdom."

If you're into abuse, pure and simple, homebrew's chief advantage is its low cost. But for real excess, I'd recommend boilermakers—chasing shots of whiskey with glasses of homebrew. You'll get a lot of alcohol fast and—especially if you mix bourbon with dark brew—you'll build yourself one hell of a hangover.

Everyone wants to give advice on hangovers. Before I get to mine, though, I'd like to warn you about (or against) everyone else's. First, never believe people who tell you that they have a *cure* for a hangover. Impossible. Neither the Second Law of Thermodynamics nor Cosmic Morality allows such a thing. It's true that you can *prevent* a hangover, but only by not abusing alcohol in the first place, and that's not what we're talking about.

(I will admit that you can lessen the impact of a hangover by taking certain measures while drinking, but all too often these measures lead away from abuse. Taking a glass of water between drinks, for example, breaks the thirst chain and rehydrates the body, but if you persist, you won't drink as much alcohol. Though flexible, your bladder has finite volume. Throwing up voluntarily removes alcohol from your stomach, but if you throw up involuntarily, it's too late for countermeasures. Taking aspirin before going to bed inhibits the formation of prostoglandins, organic compounds which, I'm told, add to the miseries. If you take aspirin to protect you from prostoglandins, I'd advise taking vitamin C to protect you from aspirin.)

Advice on what to do after you have a hangover has nothing to do with a cure either. When examined closely, all such advice boils down to merely *surviving* the hangover. Since every conceivable activity—eating, drinking, thinking, sex, sleeping, working, shirking, doing dex—is both recommended and forbidden, you can and should do whatever you think will best get you through.

But I'd like to recommend a new approach to the hangover: Enjoy It.

At some level and in some way, you wanted (or at least were willing to tolerate) a hangover. It may well be some sort of symbolical and necessary working out of the process that started you abusing alcohol. If the deathwish theorists are right, the hangover may be rebirth—with plenty of trauma. Or you may be attempting to work out or redress the old, all-American, pan-Puritan, Guilt Trip: you've had your forbidden pleasure, sucker, now you've got to, by God, *pay* for it. And, maybe, only by paying for it out of proportion will you be able to some day get off the Road and into the Palace.

Symbolical working out aside, the hangover can also be enjoyed as an Altered State of Consciousness (such as dreaming, meditating, or, in fact, drinking), which, though compounded of others, is, nonetheless, unique. Since you've probably taken on a good alcohol load and since metabolism is slowed during sleep, you still may have enough alcohol in your brain tissues to be partially drunk. Brain function is further impaired by the recent death of a few million (or billion) cells and by a slight anoxia (a common ingredient of many ASC's) caused by a lowered capacity to exchange oxygen. Finally, since alcohol suppresses dreaming, you're in a dream deprived state as well.

Can you dig it? that dragged out feeling? that utter despair? that sometimes complete belief that even if you can survive the physical discomforts of the hangover, you'd just as soon not? Sometimes the whole experience is not unlike certain (chiefly French) movies of the sixties whose main and only point was that life lacks even the dignity of pain (which, come to think of it, the hangover doesn't) and contains only ennui.

Some Mornings After, you find holes in your recollections of the Night Before. These memory blanks are thought to be caused by failure of the mind to transfer the contents of short-term memory to permanent storage. How this transfer takes place isn't fully understood, but it seems to require a delay of about twenty minutes. Therefore, if the mind shuts down (due, say, to a mild overdose of alcohol), whatever happened in the last twenty minutes of consciousness is never transferred. Transfer seems also to take place at night during periods of dreaming. Since even small amounts of alcohol interfere with dreaming, they may also be able to cause memory blanks.

Dealing with loss of memory takes a number of forms. We can go into a psychoanalytical funk. Influenced by Freud, we may feel that if we've forgotten something, it's because we've suppressed it; and if we've suppressed it, then it was painful but significant. "If I could only remember," we tell ourselves, "I'd have the key to my hangups." Since we can't, we feel discomfort and guilt.

Another approach is self-consolation: "Well, even if I can't remember what in the hell I did and no matter how bad and embarrassing it was, everybody else was so drunk that they probably didn't even notice." This approach is particularly useful when memory failure is less than complete.

But, again, why not enjoy those memory blanks? If Mr. Compson, Quentin Compson, Rosa Coldfield, Shreve McCannon, and the reader can derive aesthetic pleasure from their pursuit of what they can't know directly and can only infer about Thomas Sutpen, you should be able not only to piece together what you must have said (or done) to Mary last night from what she says today, how her husband acts, and what others tell you about it (keeping in mind that all or most of them are lying or can't remember because they were drunk, too), but also to get something out of it or out of your failure to know.

One last aspect of abuse, and we'll be done. In addition to passively experiencing the psychic effects of a hangover, you can actively explore what is happening to your body as a result of alcohol. Rather than single out details, I take a total approach: The Morning After, I get out of bed, leap on my bicycle, and take a fast, two-mile uphill run, ending at the top of an old Chinese cemetery. There, surrounded by tombstones covered with incomprehensible characters, my head throbbing, my mouth lined with leather, my lungs heaving to pump air into my oxygen-starved body, my skin at once cold and sweaty, my kidneys aching, and my legs turned to lead by accumulated fatigue toxins, I hear above the gasping of my breath one small bird singing to the morning and suddenly, more than at any other place or time, I know about the abuse of alcohol.

Appendix A

Mail-Order Outfits

I pondered for some time whether to annotate the list or not and have been faintly discouraged by the prospect of lawsuits on the part of those whom I slighted with faint praise or didn't even mention at all. Annotations won out. *Consumers' Reports* has them; the *Whole Earth Catalog* has them. What the hell is freedom of speech all about anyway?

Fairness (and maybe cowardice) prompts me to add this disclaimer: Omission from the list means nothing. Winemaking and homebrewing are increasing in popularity and the number of mail-order outfits grows all the time. These are the ones I knew about when I wrote the book.

F.H. Steinbart Co.
526 S.E. Grand Ave.
Portland, Oregon 97214

Steinbart sends a price list rather than a catalog, so you have to know a little bit about what you're doing in order to order. Prices are FOB, Portland, for the most part, but are low. Steinbart has good prices on bulk quantities and if you have some friends who are also getting into brewing you could do well on a combined order.

E.S. Kraus
P.O. Box 451
Nevada, Mo. 64772

Kraus sells postpaid and their central location must give them some kind of an advantage since their prices are good. When I have a small order, I usually send it to them. Their service is outstanding; I've received whatever I've ordered within ten days every time. Their catalog is informative as well.

Semplex of U.S.A.

Box 12276

Minneapolis, Minn. 55412

Semplex is an English outfit and, consequently, Semplex of U.S.A. carries a lot of British and continental gear. When I first got into brewing, Semplex's prices seemed high compared to others, so I didn't order from them. Later, prices got better and I now suspect that they depend on how the dollar is doing compared to the pound. Semplex ships postpaid and their catalog has some unique items and some bargains. Worth looking at.

Wine-Art

3417 W. Broadway

Vancouver, B.C. V6R 2B4

This is a franchise chain of winemaking and homebrewing supply houses with over 80 stores scattered about the United States and Canada. One may be nearer to you than anyone else. Some bargains and some unique items. You may be able to save on postage. For the address of the outlet nearest you, write to Wine-Art at the above address.

The last two outfits carry little in the way of homebrewing equipment and supplies, but their catalogs will be worthwhile to you if you're interested in winemaking.

Presque Isle Wine Cellars

9440 Buffalo Road

North East, PA 16428

Exceptionally informative catalog. Good prices.

The Winemaker's Shop

R.D. 2, Bully Hill Road

Hammondsport, NY 14840

The most beautiful catalog for anything I've ever seen.

Appendix B

IRS: Instant Respectability Service

To be respectable and law-abiding, you must complete two copies of Form 1541, Home Winemaking Permit. The quickest and simplest way to get the forms may be to look up your local IRS office in the phone book, give them a call, and see whether they have them. Since the Bureau of Alcohol, Tobacco, and Firearms was spun-off from the IRS in 1972, your local IRS may or may not have the forms in stock.

If they don't, send your request to: Bureau of Alcohol, Tobacco, and Firearms; Regional Office; and add the following street address that applies:

Region: States	Street Address
Central: MI, IN, OH, KY, WV.	550 Main St. Cincinnati, OH 45202
Mid-Atlantic: PA, NJ, DE, MD, VA.	2 Penn Center Plaza Philadelphia, PA 19102
Midwest: ND, SD, NB, MN MO, IA, WI, IL.	35 E. Wacker Dr. Chicago, IL 60601
North Atlantic: ME, VT, NH, NY, MA, CT, RI.	90 Church St. New York, NY 10007
Southeast: TN, NC, MS, AL, GA, FL, SC.	275 Peachtree St. NE Atlanta, GA 30303
Southwest: WY, CO, KS NM, OK, TX, AR, LA.	1110 Commerce St. Dallas, TX 75202

Western: WA, ID, MT, OR,   870 Market St.
CA, NV, UT, AZ, HI, AK.   San Francisco, CA 94102

They'll send you two forms with instructions, you'll fill both out and send them back, they'll stamp them, and send one of them back to you as your license and record of wine produced.

Appendix C

Tables

Hydrometer scale conversions. Do you have a single-scale hydrometer and need to know a reading in another system? Here's a conversion table:

SG	Brix	Pot. alc.
1.005	1.6	0.5
1.010	3.0	0.9
1.015	4.1	1.6
1.020	5.3	2.3
1.025	6.5	3.0
1.030	7.7	3.7
1.035	8.8	4.4
1.040	9.9	5.1
1.045	11.1	5.8
1.050	12.3	6.5
1.055	13.4	7.2
1.060	14.5	7.8
1.065	15.7	8.6
1.070	16.9	9.2
1.075	18.0	9.9
1.080	19.2	10.6
1.085	20.4	11.3

SG	Brix	Pot. alc.
1.090	21.5	12.0
1.095	22.6	12.7
1.100	23.7	13.4
1.105	24.8	14.1
1.110	25.9	14.9

Temperature corrections. Most hydrometers are calibrated at 60° F. If you're brewing at a higher temperature and are too impatient to wait for your sample to cool, use the following corrections:

Temp	Add to SG
70	.001
77	.002
84	.003
95	.005
105	.007

Appendix D

British Measurement

If you get one of the many British books on brewing, you'll find that the Britons use Imperial gallons and measure dry ingredients in pounds. If you want to try their recipes, there are two ways to go about it. First, if you use U.S. gallons and figure that one pound of sugar equals two cups, the wort will wind up with about seven percent more dry ingredients than the British recipe calls for—a negligible error (about $\frac{1}{2}$ of 1 percent *more* potential alcohol). Second, if you can weigh your dry ingredients, you can use 6 U.S. gallons (or quarts or pints) equals 5 Imperial gallons (or quarts or pints). Fluid ounces are another matter because the Imperial gallon has 160 Imperial ounces and the U.S. gallon has 128 U.S. ounces. One Imperial fluid ounce equals 28.413 milliliters. One U.S. fluid ounce equals 29.573 milliliters. The U.S. ounce is therefore four percent larger than the Imperial ounce—again, a negligible error (about $\frac{1}{4}$ of 1 percent *less* potential alcohol).

Wouldn't it be easy if we all used the metric system?

Index

Notes

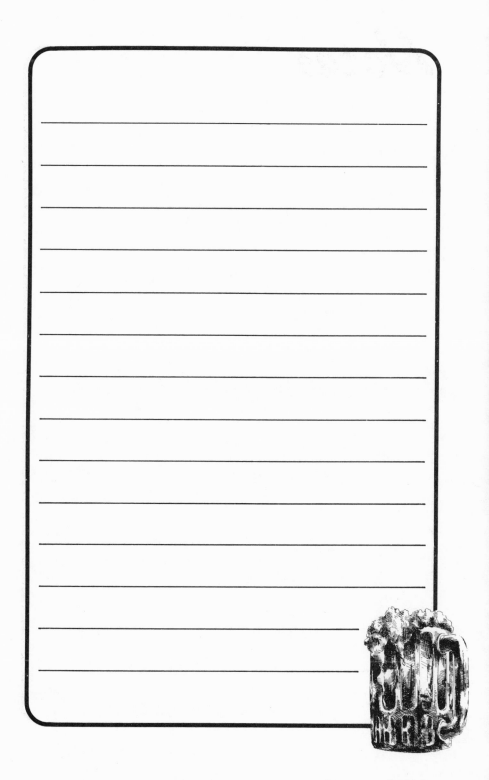

Notes

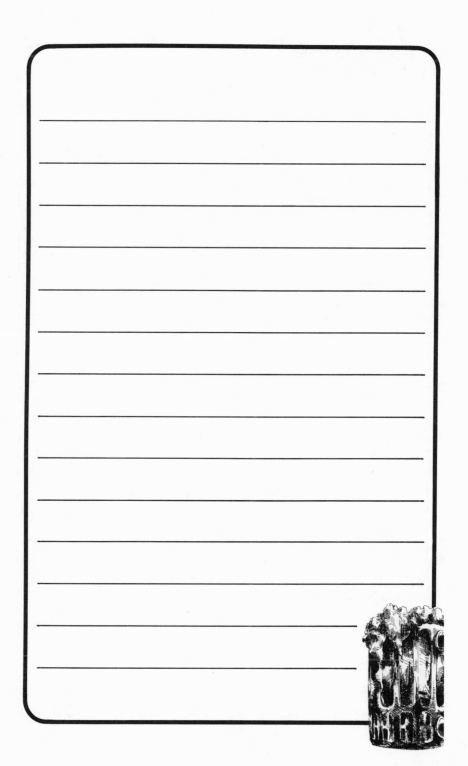

Notes

*2284-16
1980
5-43
C